WEALTH WITHOUT GUILT

Roland J. Hill, D. Min.

Helping Hands Press
P.O. Box 133
Keene, TX 76059

Edited by Ken McFarland
Cover art direction and design by Ed Guthero
Cover texture background art by Jeri Desmond

ISBN: 0-9639357-1-2

CONTENTS

Acknowledgments

Books have a persona of their own. They become living entities. As each contributor to a book gives time, energy, and personal insights, life is breathed into the written word. This book is no exception. This book breathes because of the contributions of several important persons.

Special thanks go to Ken McFarland, for editorial work and words of encouragement; to Ed Guthero, for his creative work and clear interpretation of my concepts in his cover design; to Marcus Sheffield for final copy editing; and to Wyatt Tee Walker for the inspiration to continue writing books.

I am especially grateful to Susie Hill, my wife, for her administrative leadership of this entire project. With persistence, commitment, and follow-through, she helped navigate this project to its completion.

Finally, all praise and thanksgiving go to God, who was willing to empower ordinary people to give understanding and life to the written word.

Dedication

To the many Gospel workers who have worked sacrificially in the heat of the day.

FOREWORD

Wealth Without Guilt is must reading for earnest Christians. Its importance, aside from its instructive and practical value, is that it plows new ground in contemporary Christian thought. This volume will do much to resolve the pervasive ambivalence that is present in Christian circles, on the question of money and material possessions.

The Christian Church cannot exist without money and material resources of the realm in which it exists. A two-fold continuing dilemma exists in Christian venues: 1) In what prescribed and reasonable manner shall Christian churches extract from their communicants the resources they need for ministry, and 2) how shall Christian churches inform and educate their communicants, *on biblical principles*, of appropriate personal attitudes toward money and possessions?

This dilemma is real and at many points disconcerting, especially to the African-American community, which remains at the bottom of the economic ladder in the United States.

The value of Roland Hill's study, *Wealth Without Guilt*, is that it speaks directly to this issue. He has given careful analysis to the ambiguity which prevails in the ranks of Christendom generally and in African-American church life particularly. Unlike many tomes which lift up a problem and support their critiques with substantial analysis, Dr. Hill's work offers some very concrete and viable solutions. It may not be an exaggeration to say that this book can be a blueprint for the survival of the African-American Church in the 21st century—and perhaps of the race!

The reader is admonished that this is not a *Dick-and-Jane* book. It is serious reading and will require some considerable thought and reflection in order to glean the larger harvest of its value and importance.

5

In addition to his main thrust of developing some new foundational principles for the Christian enterprise, the author provides a very careful historical record of precisely how the Christian Church developed this nettlesome ambiguity on the issue of money and possessions. The book is both informative and persuasive in its content—and careful in its scholarship and documentation.

Any Christian—clergy or layperson—will be greatly benefited from the investment made in purchasing this volume. It holds the promise of a ten- , twenty- , or hundred-fold return, in establishing in one's spirit a wholesome and theologically based attitude toward money and possessions.

Wyatt Tee Walker
Canaan Baptist Church of Christ
Harlem, New York

CHAPTER 1

WEALTH WITHOUT GUILT

Wealth! I have always wanted it—
and chances are, so have you. But like many, I have lived with a tremendous guilt complex about money and wealth. Being born into a Christian home, brought up knowing and accepting the mission of the church—that of spreading the good news about Christ—and accepting Christ and His call to ministry at an early age—all this set the stage for a long and painful struggle over what seemed to be opposing ideas. How can one desire to be rich and be a Christian too? The more I examined my motives for being wealthy, the greater the tension.

The only profession that ever appealed to me was that of being a preacher. While other children played fireman, postman, doctor, lawyer, or truck driver, I played preacher. I cut my homiletical teeth preaching atop wood crates with my sister and her dollies as members. The call I felt to the ministry was so compelling that I even practiced baptizing. With one hand in the air, and while repeating the formula used by my father as he baptized, I took my sister under imaginary water. She couldn't help being saved after being baptized so many times!

Even as I entered junior high school, my desire to imitate my father, a devoted Christian minister, was seen in how I dressed at school. No casual clothes for me. Shirt, tie, and dress shoes were all that I permitted myself to wear. There was no mistaking what I wanted be—a preacher. I looked liked a preacher and acted like a preacher.

As a teenager, women, wine, and riotous living were not my downfall. I wanted to live a pure life for Jesus, especially because of my call to the ministry. But I never dared reveal one of my deepest wishes—that of being wealthy. Even now—though I know the feelings are not legitimate, I cannot help but feel a bit ashamed and somehow "unspiritual" as I approach writing about the subject of wealth. What supposedly "spiritual" man in his right mind would desire something so carnal as money? And shouldn't preachers be concerned only with spiritual matters?

But through the years, the material needs of humanity have pressed upon my heart. I have longed to answer those needs with more than a prayer but also with profits—not just with sympathetic words but with personal wealth. But where were the preachers to resolve the tension I felt? Where were the Christian businessmen who felt good about their wealth? Where were the Bible lessons or classes that taught more than tithing, freewill offerings, sacrifice, and prudence? Where was the encouragment to increase one's personal wealth so that there could be more to sacrifice?

It seemed to me that if one were to become wealthy, it would have to be without the church's encouragement. Like so many other Christians, my guilt became heavier with church activity and attendance. Why was I feeling so guilty about wealth? Why did the church add to this guilt? Where did this come from? And was this how God wanted us to feel about wealth?

Well, my friend, this is what *Wealth Without Guilt* is all about. This book seeks to answer the questions that have arisen in my own mind about wealth and spirituality. I am sure many other elements come into play concerning the whole issue of wealth, but *Wealth Without Guilt* seeks to get at the root of the problem of guilt about wealth. My prayer is that this book will do for you what it has done for me and for the thousands of others who have attended my seminars.

CHAPTER 2

WARPED THINKING ABOUT WEALTH

The aphorism, "As a man thinketh in his heart, so is he" not only embraces all of man's being but reaches out to every condition and circumstance of his life. A man is literally what he thinks, his character being the sum of all his thoughts. But interestingly enough, treatments of the economic dilemma of Christians neglect this basic truth. Christians are seemingly viewed as machines—give them some modern tools, and they will remedy their economic dilemma.

Tools are important, but more important by far is the right attitude toward tools. A careful observation of Christian thinking about the material world reveals ambivalent and/or ambiguous attitudes. Tools and how-to books on money management alone will not effect the deeper desired changes. The economic quandary of Christians is not due simply to a lack of tools but to an inadequate mindset about tools. To assist Christians in getting beyond this economic impasse, we must begin by considering attitudinal changes.

Man is indeed a creature of his thoughts. James Allen makes this insightful statement:

Man is made or unmade by himself, in the armory of

thought he forges the weapons by which he destroys himself; he also fashions the tools with which he builds for himself heavenly mansions of joy and strength and peace. By right choice and true application of thought, man ascends to Divine Perfection; by the abuse and wrong application of thought, he descends below the level of the beast. Between these two extremes are all the grades of character, and man is their maker and master.[1]

The Christian's financial status is made or unmade by his attitude toward the material world. His thoughts are shaped by ideologies that either help or hinder him in a tightening economy. A miasma of ambiguity about the material world exists that hinders or restricts the Christian's spiritual, as well as economic, freedom. No man can rise higher than his thoughts. No goals can be reached when there is bedlam in the mind. Maxwell Maltz says that both "behaviour and feelings spring from belief."[2]

What do Christians think about the material world? It appears that many see the material world only as a necessary evil. This view contributes to old platitudes of folklore, such as: poverty is next to spirituality; to be wealthy is a sin; money is the root of all evil. But mental conflicts come into play when those same Christians read the Bible and discover a message like this—"So that this man [Job] was the greatest [wealthiest] of all the men of the east" (Job 1:3). For centuries, Christians have struggled with these conflicting views, without apparent success at resolving them.

Solomon was right when he said, "Guard your heart, for out of it flows the issues of life" (Prov. 4:23). Allen says:

> That circumstances grow out of thoughts, every man knows who has for any length of time practiced self-control and self-purification, or he will have noticed that the alteration in his circumstances has been in exact ratio with his altered mental condition.[3]

So then to hope in any way to impact the economic dilemmas Christians face requires an examination of the ideologies that have caused this ambivalence and ambiguity toward the material world. Then the

findings of this investigation must be conveyed to Christians as a means
of clearing away the miasma of ambiguity. Marvin Karlans, in his book
Persuasion, states, "Successful persuasion takes into account the reasons
for underlying attitudes as well as the attitudes themselves."[4]

For many Christians, their equivocal attitudes toward money have
resulted in a psychosis. This mental condition causes uncertainty of
action, so that Christians fear not only financial failure but also financial success.

> In the tragic separation between religion and daily life, no
> area has developed a wider gap than that between faith and
> economic affairs. . . . The result of the split has been to make
> faith irrelevant and barren and economic life sterile and with-
> out higher purpose. The unfortunate result is that men are
> compelled to live in the hazardous and complicated world of
> occupational life without a sense of sacred calling, while their
> religious lives must be lived in ghostly and disembodied de-
> tachment from the arena of action and decision.[5]

D. L. Mundy, in his book *God and the Rich Society*, sees Christians as a
group retreating from the world. He believes this is due to frustration
on the part of Christians in not knowing how to cope with the material
world.[6] Mundy is on target, because the Christian's economic dilemma
arises mainly out of a failure to deal with this problem. Mundy further
states, "But it can hardly be denied that the characteristic temptation of
our day is to give up the struggle with the world, or if we do really live
out our lives in the world, we do not struggle with it."[7]

But for those who continue struggling with seemingly conflicting
views of the material versus the spiritual, victory will only come when
ambiguous views are averted with the inoculation of pure, clear, correct
thoughts on financial matters. Christians must be told:

> Into your hands will be placed the exact results of your
> own thoughts; you will receive that which you earn; no more,
> no less. Whatever your present environment may be, you
> will fall, remain, or rise with your thought.[8]

So now we know that man is the captain of his ship, the master of his fate, but he does not live in a vacuum. Where do these conflicting ideas come from? How does one solidify his thinking on matters such as this? Socrates felt that it was necessary to create a tension in the mind so that the individual could rise from the bondage of myths and ambiguous thinking.

Truth must be pitted against error, error against truth; so that through this tension, the mind might differentiate between the two. But before we can deal with conflicting views, we must deal with how we form most of our attitudes and opinions. "A person's opinions and attitudes are strongly influenced by the groups to which he belongs and wants to belong."[9] For the Christian, attitudes and opinions are strongly influenced by the church.

Since the church plays such an important role in forming the attitudes of its members, it may be correctly inferred that the church has therefore been a major factor in helping create the ambiguous attitudes modern Christians have about money.

Notes:

1. James Allen, *As a Man Thinketh* (New York: Grosset & Dunlap, 1981), p. 5.

2. Maxwell Maltz, *Psycho-Cybernetics* (New York: Grosset & Dunlap, 1981), p. 5.

3. Allen, p. 14.

4. Marvin Karlans and Herbert I. Abelson, *Persuasion, How Opinions and Attitudes Are Changed* (New York: Springer Publisher Company, Inc.).

5. Albert T. Rasmussen, *Christian Responsibility in Economic Life* (Philadelphia: Westminster Press, 1955).

6. D. L. Mundy, *God and the Rich Society* (New York: Oxford University Press, 1961), p. 3.

7. *Ibid.*, p. 11.

8. Allen, *op. cit.*, p. 63.

9. Karlans, p. 49.

Who is Affecting Your Thinking?

We ended the last chapter with an indictment of the church for contributing to attitudes of economic ambiguity. Let us examine this indictment further. Historically, the church has been a primary source of knowledge, customs, beliefs, and ideals:

> Religion has always been one of the most powerful forces in history. Often religious teachings influence all aspects of a person's life. All religions try to offer their followers a set of values by which to live. Through stressing ethical conduct, they give people a framework for judging right from wrong and for living a good life.[1]

The Christian's worldview has been greatly influenced by the church. Thus, his attitudes about money and the material world also have been affected by the church:

> While the Christian church has no sharp moral absolutes to guide its members in the hard arena of economic decision making, it does provide something infinitely more significant. This is the fellowship of the spirit in which is generated material self-criticism and support in confronting all deci-

sion to be made. Too often the church has misrepresented itself to the outsiders in the world and consequently has been misunderstood. Instead of divine law for economic guidance, it offers provisional judgments of Christians, consisting of their very human sense of present responsibility. Under the modest claim it is the obligation of the Christian and the church to make judgments about the great issues of economic responsibility as the Holy Spirit leads and corrects them.[2]

The church knows the influence it has on its members, so it institutes teaching programs to secure the greatest impact. That is, it institutes teaching programs in most areas except economics. The area of economics has remained a neglected subject, because the church believed for more than fifteen hundred years that the world is essentially evil and that withdrawal from it is the only way to practice the authentic Christian life.

Christianity, for many centuries, has been an other-worldly religion. As mentioned earlier, there is a tragic dichotomy between religion and the daily life. Albert Rasmussen states: "The gap has been due to several radical misunderstandings of both classical Biblical Protestant faith and the process of economic activity."[3]

The church must face its historic obligation in the crisis. In the final analysis, this economic dilemma of Christians is not simply a social problem but a spiritual one as well. It has always been the responsibility of the church to broaden horizons, challenge the status quo, and break mores when necessary. The task of resolving the economic impasse of Christians is an inescapable necessity confronting the church today.

Martin Luther King, Jr., so succinctly said:

Any religion which professes to be concerned about the souls of men and is not concerned about the social and economic conditions that scar the soul, is a spiritually moribund religion only waiting for the day to be buried. It is well said, "A religion that ends with the individual, ends."[4]

Can the church stand calmly by while economic insecurity strangles the physical, cultural, and spiritual growth of its members? Emphatically, no! The church is God's appointed agency for the promulgation of the gospel, and the gospel is the good news that Jesus came to free man from spiritual and economic bondage. Did not Jesus say, "I am come that they might have life more abundantly" (John 10:10)?

> . . . churches most representative of Christian faith and witness are those that recognize that religion deals with both earth and heaven, both time and eternity. They recognize that the Christian's gospel is a two-way road. On the one hand it seeks to change the souls of men and unite them with God; on the other hand it seeks to change the conditions in which men live so that the soul will have a chance after it is changed.[5]

The church must be concerned about the economic life of its members, because economic activity and discourse lie at the very heart of human experience.

There are several things that the church can do to assist in this crisis. First, it can reaffirm its responsibility for instruction in the social aspects of the gospel. This can be done by encouraging its clergy to assert their prophetic role in the community. Rauschenbusch affirms that,

> If a minister uses the great teaching powers of the pulpit sanely and wisely to open the minds of the people to the moral importance of the social, he can be of utmost usefulness in ameliorating the social order.[6]

Martin Luther King, Jr., noting the importance of the clergy in attitudinal changes, writes, "Every minister of the gospel has a mandate to proclaim the eternal verities of the gospel, and to lead men from the darkness of falsehood and fear to the light of truth and love."[7]

Attitudinal changes must begin in the church, where they come from. For centuries ministers have preached a foggy gospel, resulting in ambiguities among Christians. Now the church must reeducate, reindoctrinate the laity through correct Scriptural truth about money and the material world. The minister who has been historically given high credibility in the community will have an enormous impact in arresting this measure of ambiguity. Karlan states, "There will be more opinion change in the desired direction if the communicator has high credibility than if he has low credibility."[8]

Secondly, the church must get to the ideological roots of economic ambiguity. All ambiguities come out of a struggle between conflicting ideologies. The church can be of immeasurable help in giving the confused Christian the needed right direction. Through the channel of religious education, the church can point out the myths and false philosophies—and show the correct view.

Thirdly, and finally, the church can end its dichotomous lifestyle. The church has talked out of both sides of its mouth. While it has condemned the material world, it has bathed in luxury. While its coffers have grown fat, the church has encouraged Christians to shun the world. Not only must the church teach a correct view toward the material world; it also must live it. Paul says, "Be ye followers of me as I follow Christ" (I Cor. 4:16). The church must offer not only an *audio* presentation, but also a *video* presentation of God's expectations for us in the material world.

The church has a grave responsibility as it relates to the economic well-being of Christians. Many influences seek to shape the thinking of Christians, which we will discuss in the next chapter, but the church has the upper hand. It should use its great influence to put Christians on the road to financial freedom.

Notes:

1. World Book, 1968 ed., Q-R volume 16 (Chicago, Illinois: Field Enterprises Educational Corporation, 1968 ed.), pp. 207, 214.

2. Albert T. Rasmussen, *Christian Responsibility in Economic Life* (Philadelphia: Westminster Press, 1955), p. 88.

3. *Ibid.*, p. 4.

4. Martin Luther King, Jr., *Strides Toward Freedom*, The Montgomery Story (New York: Harper & Brothers, 1968), p. 91.

5. Rasmussen, *op. cit.*, p. 138.

6. Ervin Smith, *The Ethics of Martin Luther King, Jr.* (Lewiston, NY: The Edwin Mellen Press, 1981), p. 136.

7. King, *op. cit.*, p. 208.

8. Marvin Karlans and Herbert I. Abelson, *Persuasion, How Opinions and Attitudes Are Changed* (New York: Springer Publisher Company, Inc.), p. 108.

CHAPTER 4

WHO LEAVES THE BIBLE OUT?

Learning to think biblically should be one of the Christian's major ambitions. This objective is not easy to attain, since we are almost constantly influenced by nonbiblical philosophies and standards. Because it is not natural for us to think biblically, we need not be alarmed if much of our thinking is molded by the non-Christian world around us. This is not to say that non-Christian influences have been all good or all bad, but only to recognize that our thinking has been affected by them. When we grasp this fact, then our eyes are opened to the task of reeducating ourselves to break away from the non-Christian philosophies that conflict with Bible truth.

Christian thought, to a great extent, has been shaped by Greek thought and philosophies. Freeman Butts, in his book *Cultural History of Western Education*, says, "We think the way we do in large part because the Greeks thought the way they did."[1]

It is important for Christian educators to face this issue squarely for a number of reasons. First, Greek intellectualism with its consequent scientific naturalism is definitely the intellectual context within which many in Christian education work. Second, this subject is relevant because Christian education has had the tendency to compromise with the context. Third, many of our Christian teachers, while subscribing clearly to orthodox theological positions and enjoying genuine Christian experience, have been so steeped in this context that it is hard for them to break away from its premises in the classroom.[2]

What is true for the Christian classroom holds true also for Christian economic thinking. Christian economic thought has been so shaped by Greek thought that it is difficult at times to differentiate between the two.

Other systems of thought have had an effect on Christian thought, but none has had as much impact as Greek thought. So, for our purposes here, we shall only examine Greek thought.

The Greeks are purported to have been the first people to ask, "What is life's true reality?" To Plato, life's true reality centered only on the Perfect One—God.[3]

Plato, because of constant striving for moral and social perfection and because of his other-worldly views, is sometimes called a Christian before Christ, but we shall examine in the next chapter how his other-worldly thinking has wrought havoc in Christian economic thinking.

Another philosophical view that has left scars on Christian thinking is the "this-worldliness" of the Sophist. This is the polar opposite of Plato's other-worldliness. Again following in the true spirit of the ancient Greeks, the Sophist advocated a form of thinking called reasoning:

> They maintained that metaphysical issues were beyond solution; therefore, scholars should concentrate on human nature and human relations. They became famous for their statement, "Man is the measure of all things." They were concerned with the sense world and used reason as a tool to achieve success in that world.[4]

So, in Greek thought, Plato forms the thesis and the Sophist the antithesis. It would seem natural that someone would come along to bring a compromise between the two. Aristotle provided what he felt was a synthesis between the two divergent views. His metaphysic is summed up in his views on form and matter:

> Matter is by nature purposeless. Form is mind or spirit at work transforming matter into something that has life and purpose, it is creative, active and purposive. His form is close to Plato's "ideas," but not quite the same. In fact, he arrives through the famous doctrine of theorice, the undisturbed meditation on God, at God who is the unmoved mover, the Final Cause.[5]

Aristotle's synthesis has been attractive to Christian thought, because life for him was not a dead end but rather a striving toward a better end. Taking in the whole gamut of Greek thought, Brinton, in his book *Ideas and Man* reveals the Greek influence on Christian thinking:

> 1. This life and this world, not the world beyond death, is prominent.

> 2. The satisfaction of natural human desires and needs is the primary motivation for living.

> 3. "Nothing in excess" established the principle of discipline and control in life process, the Golden Mean of Aristotle.

> 4. Intelligent competition provided good motivation for one to do his best at anything worth doing.[6]

Brinton is not at all enthusiastic about Greek thought, however. He points out that the Greek was earthbound, tied to sensual experience, without hope of immortality, and with no belief in a God morally interested in his fate. And although the Greek had some sense of right and wrong, he had no feelings equivalent to what is meant by a sense of sin.

These Greek philosophies have played an enormous part in shaping Christians' attitudes toward the world. But we must not conclude that Greek philosophies were readily accepted by Christians. In fact, in the next chapter, we will discuss the struggle between Greek philosophy and Christian thought and discover how Greek philosophy fared.

Notes:

1. Freeman Butts, *Cultural History of Western Education* (New York: McGraw-Hill Book Company, Inc., 1955), p. 45.

2. H. W. Byrne, *A Christian Approach to Education* (Grand Rapids, MI: Zondervan Publishing House, 1961), p. 17.

3. *Ibid.*, p. 18.

4. *Ibid.*

5. *Ibid.*

6. Crane Brinton, *Ideas and Man* (Englewood Cliffs, NJ: Prentice Hall, 1950), p. 65.

WHERE DID GUILT ABOUT WEALTH COME FROM?

Greek thought, which has had so much impact on the church, came mainly through Gnosticism, which was and is the most dangerous and penetrating "ism" influencing the church. This is because Gnosticism was a syncretism of Greek, heathen, and Judaistic thought. Henry Chadwick, in *The Early Church*, states, "The conquest of Gnosticism may be counted the hardest and most decisive battle in church history."[1] William Hordern stated:

> The first great heresy, Gnosticism, arose in the second and third centuries. It was a movement that threatened Christianity from within at the time when the Roman emperors were threatening it from without, and of the two threats, Gnostics were the most dangerous.[2]

The Gnostics were philosophers who wished to amalgamate all religions of the world by eclectically choosing the best from each of them. But the aspect of Gnosticism that has most influenced Christian thinking to our detriment is Gnostic dualism:

> Perhaps its most fundamental conception, the wholly evil character of the phenomenal world, was due to a combina-

tion of the platonic theory of the contrast between the real spiritual sphere of "ideas," and this visible world of phenomena, interpreted in terms of Persian dualism, the good and that which man strives to return, the other wholly bad and the place of his imprisonment. The world of matter is evil.[3]

The Gnostic believed that man's highest aim must be the redemption of the body from the world of matter. This was completely opposite from the Judaistic view of redemption, which was the redemption of mankind from sin. Starting from this idea that matter is always sinful, including man's body, the Gnostic maintained that the divine nature was utterly alien to the material world. Marianne H. Micks says:

> When one believes that material things, including the physical body, are either evil or illusory, two quite opposite attitudes toward them are possible. On the one hand, one can logically decide that they are insignificant, that what one does with his body, for example, is of no great importance. This results in an ethical indifference, the position of the antinomian, who is above the law. On the other hand, with equal logic, one can decide that the physical side of his life must be rigidly controlled, and adopt all sorts of ascetic practices to insure the mastery of the material by the spiritual.[4]

Out of the dualism of Gnosticism came the twin enemies of biblical truth: materialism and spiritualism.

Materialists viewed external acts as not affecting the inner devotion of the mind. This group became notorious for their arguments favoring immorality and a general lack of restraint for the body. The book of Jude warns against one such Gnostic group which was exploiting the agape or love feast and turning it into an occasion of riotous license.

Spiritualists were those who denied the value of physical realities. This led to an ascetic life with rules for mortification of the flesh and a special prohibition on marriage (or at least on procreation), so that the divine soul might be liberated from the bonds of sense and bodily appetite and assisted to turn itself toward higher things.

Spiritualism was accepted by the majority of the different Gnostic groups. And it is spiritualism—asceticism—that has been the main cause of the ambiguous feelings contributing to the economic dilemma Christians face.

Asceticism, "the religious doctrine that one can reach a higher spiritual state by rigorous self-discipline and self-denial,"[5] can be traced as it has woven its way through church history.

The earliest mention of the penetration of Gnostic asceticism was among a Jewish protest group called the Essenes. The Essenes were a rigidly separated group living a semi-monastic life. Their lives were frugal—any member who had two coats gave one away to his brother and wore his remaining coat until it was threadbare. They did not condemn marriage as wrong, but they did expect full members of the community to be celibate. Chadwick states, "... perhaps the Greek documents present a portrait of the Essenes that reshape their likeness to resemble Pythagorean ascetics of the Hellenistic world."[6]

In the early part of the first century, Gnostic asceticism crept into Judaism. At the same time, Christianity was beginning.

During the first century, the early church was basically a pure, Bible-believing group. The church drew its followers from among the Jews and was thus influenced by Judaistic thought.

Judaism had a profound impact on Christianity, because the first Christians were indeed Jews. The distinction came only because of the fact that the Christian Jews accepted Jesus of Nazareth as the Messiah.

So for the better part of the first century, the Christian church viewed the world as did the Jewish nation—as created by God and, therefore, intrinsically good.

> The Talmud emphatically repeats the Biblical affirmation of this world and interprets the words of Genesis, "and God saw everything that He had made and behold it was very good," as referring to both worlds. The good things of this world, including sensual pleasures, may be enjoyed simply and naturally. Only in rare instances do we find any ascetic

tendencies. Even more important is the fact that asceticism plays no role in understanding of ethics. Although the moral act was understood as a preparation for the future world, it lacked the negative connotation of separation from the world of senses. Its meaning was wholly positive: to serve God in this world, to fulfill His will, and to build a social order in accordance with His will.[7]

But as the church witnessed rapid growth in the latter part of the first and second centuries, it was faced with its most difficult battles. Many diverse groups became a part of the church, bringing with them their heathen customs and nonbiblical world views. All of the different groups had been affected by Greek philosophy, with one main philosophical view dominating—that of Gnostic dualism.

Gnostic dualism brought the church into conflict with both the antinomians living unrestrained and immoral lives and the ascetic groups who protested the antinomians and the evil world.

> Ascetic ideals and a double standard of Christian morality had long been growing in the church before the time of Constantine. Their progress was aided by the ascetic tendencies inherent in the better philosophies of the ancient world. . . .The low condition of the church, emphasized by the influx of vast numbers in the peace from 260 to 303, and the conversion of Constantine, led to enlarged valuation of the ascetic life by serious-minded Christians. The cessation of martyrdoms left asceticism the highest Christian achievement attainable. The world was filled with sights that offended Christian morality, from which it seemed well to flee.[8]

During this period, the church saw the need of solidifying itself to combat this forceful attack by Gnostic dualism. Walker states:

> The circumstance of the time, the contest with Gnostics and Montanists, the leadership of increasing masses of ignorant recent converts from heathenism, the necessities of uniformity in worship and discipline, all tended to centralize in the bishop the right and authority which in earlier periods had been more widely shared.[9]

But what the church sought to rid itself of through organization came back in another form. The centralization of power, the increased formalism of public worship, as developed by the close of the third century, led to a desire for a freer and more individual approach to God. Out of this came Monasticism, the Christian brand of Gnostic asceticism. R. C. Sproul states:

> Plato's valuing of the soul over the body, the idea over the imperfect copy, has had an enormous influence on Christian thought. Consider, for example, the chapter of monastic history where austere forms of rigorous self-denial, self-flagellation, and other forms of asceticism were elevated to the status of exalted virtues because of their anti-physical and therefore "spiritual" bent.[10]

From the third century through the entire Middle Ages, this Gnostic view reigned. The church taught that the purpose of life was not to get ahead or to accumulate wealth and property, but to obey God's will according to the instruction of the church. Making money was looked upon by the church as a form of antisocial behavior and thus a sin against the divine order.

But a dichotomy existed. The peasants were consigned to eternal poverty, while the church, in cahoots with the institutions of feudalism, accumulated vast amounts of property and wealth, enjoying a life of luxury.

Wallace K. Ferguson, in *A Survey of European Civilization*, writes:

> The clergy were not far behind the nobles in exploiting the peasants. Sure, they did not rob and kill, as the nobles did in time of war, and they did much to aid the peasants by checking the lawlessness of feudal warfare. But they were one of the two privileged classes whom it was the duty of the peasants to support, and they clung tenaciously to their rights. The parish priests were often merciless in collecting their tithes, and seldom hesitated to use the dread threat of excommunication to force payment. Moreover, the church held a great deal of land, and ecclesiastical lords, in general, were no more lenient with their peasants than were the nobles.[11]

In contrasting the condition of the peasants to that of the church, Ferguson writes:

> The Roman Catholic Church in France owned approximately one-fifth of the land. Its income was enormous, one-half as great as the royal revenues, according to some estimates, and was derived from two main sources. The estates of the church brought in the equivalent of $200,000,000 a year and a sum almost as large was furnished by the tithe. This tax, theoretically one-tenth, but in practice more often one-fifteenth or less, commonly was levied upon the annual yield from land cultivated by laymen. The church itself paid no taxes to the king on its property, but the clergy voted free gifts to the royal exchequer from time to time as a scanty substitute. Part of the revenue of the church went for charitable purposes, part as salary for 130,000 clergy.[12]

The peasants could not long endure such inequities, and their growing discontent finally found expression in the Peasants' Revolt of 1381. But the time was not right for a complete change in the economic system. Though the secular world had begun to change, the church had not made any real changes. Her attitudes toward the material world were basically the same, and unless she changed, society couldn't. This was because the church was the dominant force in society. Yet a change had to come. The Reformation brought that change. Ferguson writes:

> The most obvious cause of the Reformation was the necessity of reforming abuses in the church, a necessity that had been widely recognized for the past two centuries or more, without much being done about it. The wealth and temporal power of the church; the special jurisdiction of ecclesiastical and papal courts; the appointment of foreign papal favorites to high ecclesiastical offices; the avarice, carelessness, ignorance, and immorality of some of the clergy; the evil of simony, and the financial exaction of papacy — all these served to arouse a strong feeling of discontent with the church as it was, particularly when they bore heavily on the purses of the laity.[13]

Of course, the fact that there were abuses in the church would not in itself have caused such a widespread revolt from the Roman communion as took place in the Reformation. As mentioned before, society had taken on a new dimension, and more people were prepared to break with the church than before. Ferguson explains:

> In other ways the changing spirit of the new age was causing men, especially of the bourgeois class, to lose interest in the beliefs, ideals, and traditions of the medieval church. The medieval ideal of the truly religious life, as embodied in monasticism, had stressed poverty, asceticism, and other-worldliness as among the prime virtues. But with increasing prosperity, money was playing a much more important part in men's lives, and by the beginning of the sixteenth century, the age in which St. Francis of Assisi had sung the praises of his Lady Poverty and had enrolled enthusiastic recruits in her service, had long passed.
>
> Practical businessmen had begun to think of poverty as a social evil rather than as saintly virtue. Other-worldliness made small appeal to men absorbed in the business of this world, asceticism had few charms for the hard-working burgher who looked forward soberly to an old age spent in quiet enjoyment of the results of honest trade.... Next to monasticism the strongest force in shaping the spirit was wealth, as the form of the medieval church had been feudalism. And as feudalism lost vitality, the medieval church lost the social atmosphere that had been most congenial to it.[14]

The stage was set for the great Protestant Reformation. And the Reformation brought an answer to the dichotomy.

Martin Luther, the great reformer, loosened the grasp of asceticism on the church. In 1517, he nailed his theses to the church door in Wittenberg, Germany, and changed the course of history. This was a religious document. Its sole attempt was to make the church aware of its doctrinal error. Luther lived in a time when the Roman Catholic Church and the political institutions of feudalism held sovereign sway over the life of Western Europe. For those who lived during this epoch, it seemed inconceivable that the theocentric order of the Middle Ages would ever come to an end; that the church, with its tight hold on every facet of life—social, political, economical, and spiritual— would ever come to an end. Yet Luther's doctrine led the church back to the path of a biblical worldview.

Luther's theses came out of his rage over indulgences. Malancthon expressed Luther's reaction to the indulgences this way:

> Indulgences were being hawked for sale in these parts by a most impudent Dominican sycophant, Tetzel. Irritated by the man's impious and wicked sermons and burning with zeal for godliness, Luther published his *Propositions On Indulgences*.[15]

In his theses, Luther attacked not so much indulgences themselves as their abuse. He was against the church using them as a means of salvation. Luther wrote to Albert of Mainz:

> No man can be assured of his salvation by an episcopal function. He is not even assured of his salvation by the infu- sion of God's grace, because the Apostle Paul orders us to work out our salvation constantly "in fear and trembling" (Phil. 2:12). Even "the just will hardly be saved" (1 Peter 4:18). Finally, the way that leads to life is so narrow that the Lord, through the prophets Amos and Zechariah, calls those that will be saved "a brand plucked out of the fire" (Amos 4:11; Zech. 3:2). And everywhere else the Lord proclaims the dif- ficulty of salvation. How can the indulgence agents then make people feel secure and without fear concerning salvation by means of those false stories and promises of pardon? After all, the indulgences contribute absolutely nothing to the sal- vation and holiness of souls; they only compensate for the external punishment which — on the basis of Canon Law — they once used to impose. Works of piety and love are infi- nitely better than indulgences.[16]

Luther's struggles over indulgences emerged from his conviction that a man is saved through faith and not works. He had struggled with this for years himself, finding no satisfaction in the sacraments, prayer, fast- ing, or ascetic practices of monasticism. But as he studied the works of

Augustine and Paul's Epistle to the Romans, he found satisfaction for his soul in the words "the just shall live by faith." It was out of this conviction—the just shall live by faith—that the good works of the church, feasts, pilgrimages, and even the sacraments, were seen as unnecessary, and that no man was dependent upon the services of pope or priest for his salvation. Luther's protest did not end with indulgences, but struck at other abuses of the church as well. One in particular was monasticism. He writes:

> There is another article of their unbelief: they divide the Christian life into a state of perfection and a state of imperfection; to themselves, a life of perfection. And they measure this difference not by spirit, faith, and love, which are certainly markedly predominant among ordinary people. They measure it by the show and appearance of outward works and by their vows, in which there is nothing at all, neither Spirit, faith, nor love. In fact, they destroy the spirit of faith and love. With a living faith the state of perfection despises death, life, glory, and all the world, and serves all men in fervent love.[17]

It was no doubt these views that brought about the decline of asceticism and the authority of the church. Rifkin states:

> Luther's proclamation directly challenged three underlying assumptions from which the church derived its power and authority over the Christian world: first, that church authority was equal to Biblical authority in translating God's will in matters of doctrine and policy; second, that individual salvation could be earned in this world by a combination of good works and papal intervention; and third, that the church represented the exclusive priesthood of God's chosen apostles on earth.[18]

For Luther, there was only one way to secure salvation—by faith alone. Salvation, to Luther, was a free gift from God. Only by standing alone before God in recognition of one's total depravity could the believer hope for saving grace. This teaching had the effect of undermining the church's central role in the life of the believer.

By challenging the Thomistic doctrine of grace through reason and good works, Luther also was challenging the authority of the priesthood:

> Luther undermined the authority of the church. He replaced the nation of exclusive priesthood of the church with the nation of the universal priesthood of all believers. He undermined church doctrine by proclaiming the Bible (not the Pope) as the ultimate authority in determining God's will. And, finally, leaving nothing whatsoever to human authority alone, he argued that doing good works or exercising superior reason were futile exercises, salvation did not depend on human accomplishments or abilities but only on God's grace.[19]

These Lutheran teachings unwittingly struck at the heart of the medieval society. As individuals were taught to obey their religious consciences, they made their own social interests more important than the obligation placed on them by the church. This individualism gave rise to the changes in economic thought.

But interestingly enough, Luther was not prepared for the great impact that his doctrines would have on the rank and file of the church. The peasants' lot had long been one of increasing misery and subsequent unrest. With Luther challenging the authority of the church, they felt well able to do likewise:

> In March 1525, the peasants put forth twelve articles, demanding the right of each community to choose and depose its pastor, that the great tithes (on grain) be used for the support of the pastor and community expenses, the small tithes abolished, that serfdom be done away, reservation for hunting restricted the use of the forests allowed to the poor, forced labor be regulated and duly paid, just rents fixed, new laws as loner enacted, common land restored to communities for which they had been taken and payments for inheritance to their masters abolished.[20]

Luther's first reaction over the peasant revolts was dubious, but as the peasants grew more antagonistic and appeared to become anarchistic, he turned on the peasants. It was, in large measure, Luther's earlier views that had brought about the revolts. But Luther had changed. He had come to distrust the common man, and on his advice, the proposals of the peasants were rejected.[21]

Thirty years after Luther's protest at Wittenberg, Calvin, who had been greatly influenced by Martin Luther, gave Protestantism the rigorous character of a new age of intense Puritan asceticism. Asceticism, which did not die out even with the Lutheran movement, touched on a new form.

The Puritans wished to purify the church of the remnants of Catholic ritual and to practice a simpler, holier life. Calvin was a Puritan, in the sense that he carried on the movement that had been started by the Albigenses, Waldenses, Luther, Zwingli, and others. But his work was more intense. As a reformer, he brought with him training in the classics, the mastery of French prose, and legal training. He used these tools to formulate a complete system of doctrine. Calvin's complete theological works were circulated in book form, known as *Institutes of the Christian Religion*. It was Calvin's *Institutes* that had such a great impact on the world.

Calvin, of all the reformers, brought a balance to Christian thinking. Most of the other Puritan groups left the Roman Catholic Church, but held to asceticism. The Albigenses and the Waldenses are a prime examples of this. Ferguson states:

> The former, who were also called Cathari, were the most numerous and made their appearance as early as the eleventh century. Their central doctrine seems to have been a very literal and rather morbid identification of everything physical or material with the forces of evil in the universe.
>
> This led to the rejection of all material symbols of religion—sacraments, crosses, relics, or images—and extreme asceticism, at least among the inner circle . . . who were sworn to abstain from marrying, owning property, eating flesh, or shedding blood.[22]

Ferguson does state that the Waldenses seem to have been much more orthodox, and their doctrines were closer to true Christianity. Even Luther, as has been mentioned, was not against the ascetic life-style, but against looking to it for salvation. Calvin clearly elucidated the teaching of the Bible on the material world and how we are to relate to it. In speaking about the material world, he wrote:

> But let believers accustom themselves to a contempt of the present life that engenders no hatred of it or ingratitude against God. Indeed, this life, however crammed with infinite miseries it may be, is still rightly to be counted among those blessings of God which are not to be spurned. Therefore, if we recognize in it no divine benefit, we are already guilty of grave ingratitude toward God himself. For believers especially, this ought to be a testimony of divine benevolence, wholly destined, as it is to promote their salvation. For before he shows us openly the inheritance of eternal glory, God wills by lesser proofs to show himself to be our Father. These are the benefits that are daily conferred on us by him. Since, therefore, this life serves us in understanding God's goodness, should we despise it as if it had no grain of good in itself? We must, then, become so disposed and minded that we count it among those gifts of divine generosity which are not at all to be rejected. For if testimonies of Scriptures were lacking, and they are very many and very clear, nature itself also exhorts us to give thanks to the Lord because he has brought us into its light, granted us the use of it, and provided all the necessary means to preserve it.[23]

For Calvin, Gnostic dualism had been proven false. Thus we see that Calvin's work helped rid the church of the ambiguous teaching that had held it in bondage for over fifteen hundred years. Calvin struck a deadly blow to asceticism when he wrote:

> Let this be our principle: that the use of God's gifts is not wrongly directed when it is referred to that end to which the Author himself created and destined them for us, since he created them for our good and not for our ruin. Accordingly, no one will hold to a straighter path than he who diligently looks

32

to this end. Now if we ponder to what end God created food, we shall find that he meant not only to provide for necessity but also for delight and good cheer. Thus the purpose of clothing, apart from necessity, was comeliness and decency. In grasses, trees, and fruits, apart from their various uses, there is beauty of appearance and pleasantness of odor. For if this were not true, the prophet would not have reckoned them among the benefits of God, "The wine gladdens the heart of man, the oil makes his face shine," (Psalm 104:15). Scripture would not have reminded us repeatedly, in commending his kindness, that he gave all such things to men. And the natural qualities themselves of things demonstrate sufficiently to what end and extend we may enjoy them. Has the Lord clothed the flowers with the great beauty that greets our eyes, the sweetness of smell that is wafted upon our nostrils, and yet will it be unlawful for our eyes to be affected by that beauty, or our sense of smell by the sweetness of the odor? What? Did he not so distinguish colors as to make some more lovely than others? What? Did he not endow gold and silver, ivory and marble, with a loveliness that renders them more precious than other metals or stones? Did he not, in short, render many things attractive to us, apart from their necessary use?[24]

Calvin freed us from Gnostic thinking by his clear teaching about the material world, and he set us on the road to economic freedom with his doctrine of predestination.

Calvin taught the doctrine of double predestination. He reasoned that God is in no way influenced by what each person does in the world. Since God arbitrarily chooses to save some people but not all, then salvation must, in fact, be predetermined. The natural question to follow such a belief would be, how can one know if one is among the elect? Calvin argued that no one can ever really know. Only God knows who will be saved and who will be damned. Since the world and everything in it has been organized to serve the glory of God, those who have been saved are literally programmed to fulfill the divine commandments. Calvin taught that everyone has an obligation to believe they are chosen. Jeremy Rifkin, in *The Emerging Order*, states:

That belief, according to Calvin, must be constantly renewed through the performance of God's will in the world. Constant performance and resistance to the temptation of the devil are a kind of partial proof or at least a sign that one can look to for hope that he has been saved. Parenthetically, the chief temptation of the devil is idolatry of the flesh. Sensual pleasures, music, art, dance, and all other forms of enjoyment were looked upon as evil diversions, designed to seduce the individual away from the proper performance of God's will.[25]

Rifkin was right in seeing Calvin as a double-predestinationalist, for Calvin himself says:

Indeed many, as if they wished to avert a reproach from God, accept election in such terms as to deny that anyone is condemned. But they do this very ignorantly and childishly, since election itself could not stand except as set over against reprobation. God is said to set apart those who he adopts into salvation; it will be highly absurd to say that other acquire by chance or obtain by their own effort what election alone confers on a few. Therefore, those whom God passes over, he condemns; and this he does for no other reason than that he wills to exclude them from the inheritance which he predestines for his own children. And men's insolence is unbearable; it refuses to be bridled by God's Word, which treats of his incomprehensible plan that the angels themselves adore.

However, we may have now been taught that hardening is in God's hand and will, just as much as mercies. And Paul does not, as do those I have spoken of, labor anxiously to make false excuses in God's defense; he only warns that it is unlawful for the clay to quarrel with its potter. Now how will those who do not admit that any are condemned by God dispose of Christ's statements: "Every tree that my... Father has not planted will be uprooted?" (Matthew 15:13) This plainly means that all those whom the Heavenly Father has not deigned to plant as sacred trees in his field are marked and

intended for destruction. If they say this is no sign of reprobation there is nothing so clear that it can be proved to them.[26]

R. C. Sproul, a Calvinist scholar, in *Soli Deo Gloria*, writes:

> In the Reformed view God from all eternity decrees some
> to election and positively intervenes in their lives to work
> regeneration and faith by a monergistic work of grace. To
> the non-elect God withholds this monergistic work of grace,
> passing them by and leaving them to themselves. In this view
> predestination is double in that it involved both election and
> reprobation but is not symmetrical with respect to the mode
> of divine activity. A strict parallelism of operation is denied.[27]

But Rifkin was incorrect with his implication of asceticism in Calvin's
teachings. Calvin's doctrines did influence many ascetic Puritan groups,
but he himself was not ascetic, as we have pointed out previously.

Abraham Kuyper, in *Lectures on Calvinism*, writes:

> Especially in its antithesis to Anabaptism, Calvinism ex-
> hibits itself in bold relief. For Anabaptism adopted the oppo-
> site method, and in its effort to evade the world it confirmed
> the monastic starting point, generalizing and making it a rule
> for all believers. It was not from Calvinism, but from this
> anabaptistic principle, that Akosmism had its rise among so
> many Protestants in Western Europe... Hence, on the same
> grounds on which Calvinism rejected Rome's theory concern-
> ing the world, it rejected the theory of the Anabaptist, and
> proclaimed that the Church must withdraw again within its
> spiritual domain, and that in the world we should realize the
> potencies of God's common grace.[28]

The sectarian groups of Europe, the Pietists and Anabaptists, were
influenced alike by Calvin. Many of these groups came to America, bringing with them the Calvinist tradition. They also cherished the virtues
of asceticism, frugality, and honest labor as a divine calling. All Protestantism in America has been thus influenced. Such groups as the Puritans, Quakers, Methodists, Baptists, and others shared the Calvinist tradition.

The point is that asceticism has never been destroyed in the church. It still wreaks havoc among Christians, leaving us with the miasma of ambiguity. Richardson says:

> The old name of this ancient heresy has passed away, but many of the ideas of Gnosticism reappear continually and remain in the church to this day. There is nothing particularly godly in connection with self-imposed asceticism. Something is very wrong with a Christian asceticism that will not allow God's people to enjoy and use God's gifts.[29]

Richardson continues:

> In every age there seems to be some influenced by this false idea concerning spirituality. Such spirituality, observes Dr. James I. Packer, is in no way Christian. Yet is appears constantly in the Christian church. It is evident from their behavior that to take any interest or pleasure in material things is inevitably sinful.[30]

So we see how asceticism has woven itself into the church all the way from the first to the twentieth century. If we hope to resolve the economic dilemma of Christians, we must continue the fight against Gnosticism and Gnostic influences.

Notes:

1. Henry Chadwick, *The Early Church* (London: Cox & Wyman, Ltd., 1967), p. 286.

2. William E. Hordern, *A Layman's Guide to Protestant Theology* (New York: The MacMillan Company, 1973), p. 10.

3. Williston Walker, *A History of the Christian Church* (New York: Charles Scribner & Sons, 1958), p. 52.

4. Marianne H. Micks, *Introduction to Theology* (New York: Seabury Press, Inc., 1967), p. 73.

5. *Webster's New World Dictionary of the American Language*, College Edition (1968), s.v. "Asceticism."

6. Micks, p. 74..

7. Julius Guttman, *Philosophies of Judaism* (New York: Holt, Rinehart and Winston, Inc., 1964), pp. 34, 35.

8. Chadwick, p. 14..

9. Walker, p. 125.

10. R. S. Sproul, Jr., *Money Matters* (Wheaton, IL: Tyndale House Publishers, 1985), pp. 24, 25.

11. Wallace K. Ferguson, *A Survey of European Civilization* (Boston: Houghton Mifflin Company, 1964), p. 357.

12. *Ibid.*, p. 563.

13. *Ibid.*, p. 357.

14. *Ibid.*, p. 359.

15. Kurt Alano, *Martin Luther's 95 Theses* (St. Louis, Miss.: Concordia Publishing House, 1967), p. 46.

16. *Ibid.*, p. 64.

17. *Ibid.*, p. 65.

18. Jeremy Rifkin and Ted Howard, *The Emerging Order* (New York: G.P. Putnam & Sons, 1979), p. 15.

19. Rifkin and Howard, p. 17.

20. Walker, p. 316.

21. *Ibid.*, p. 314.

22. Ferguson, p. 246.

23. John T. McNeil, *Calvin: Institutes of the Christian Religion* (Philadelphia: The Westminster Press, 1975), p. 714.

24. *Ibid.*, p. 715.

25. Rifkin and Howard, p. 19.

26. McNeil, p. 717.

27. Abraham Kuyper, *Lectures on Calvinism* (Grand Rapids, Mich.: William B. Eerdmans Publishing Co., 1966), p. 75.

28. Kuyper, pp. 3-31.

29. John R. Richardson, *Christian Economics* (Houston, Tex.: St. Thomas Press, 1960), p. 4.

30. *Ibid.*, p. 3.

CHAPTER 6

THE RESULTS OF WARPED THINKING

Gnosticism not only penetrated the church—it also had a great impact on the whole of society. Until the Reformation, society was under a theocratic government and economic system. The granting of power to the church by Constantine ended in a politically forced alliance between the pope and the emperor. Thus, all society was regulated by a set of theological absolutes, which controlled the economic world order.

The great Protestant Reformation altered this dominant theocentric world view, ushering in not only a new order of society, but also a whole new economic order. Yet the church's influence was felt even in the new order of things. The Gnostic philosophies that had impacted Christian economic thought now gravitated to the new secular economic systems that developed out of the Reformation.

Capitalism was the first economic system to emerge from the Reformation. Calvin's doctrine of unceasing activity in the performance of God's will formed the basis for the capitalistic enterprise. This doctrine resulted in Calvinists producing and accumulating more than their austere sensibilities would permit them to consume. Therefore, they took the balance and either gave it to charity or reinvested it for industrial expansion. Jeremy Rifkin, in *The Emerging Order*, which investigates the roots of capitalism, writes:

> With the Reformation person producing more than he needed to sustain his own natural physical needs, what was to become of the surplus? Calvin provided the answer. Since the surplus was never intended for the benefit of the individual but only to serve the glory of God, it would be sinful to lavish it on one's carnal appetites. On the other hand, there was nothing sinful about the surplus itself. How could there be, since it was produced to serve God's glory. Therefore, the only proper thing to do with the surplus was to reinvest it into one's calling in order to continue to improve the output and provide even larger surpluses for God's glory, and so on. Here the notion of capital formation, the key ingredient of capitalist development, was given birth.[1]

A new social class came out of the Calvinist movement. Called the *bourgeoisie*, this middle class sought to justify and spur on its own desire for material accumulation and social power. This group transformed the religious doctrines of Luther and Calvin and formulated a revolutionary new philosophy of society—liberalism. Rifkin again states:

> The bourgeoisie of the sixteenth and seventeenth centuries rebelled against the constricting tradition of feudalism. They were not interested in perpetuating an organic, static society that allowed no place for their class interests in the social order. The bourgeois, was above all else, an economic man who saw only the positive personal and social good as a result of making money. A trader or merchant by profession, he felt constrained by medieval regulations and a value system that denied the virtue of pursuing wealth for its own sake. In opposition to mercantilism, the bourgeois argued for free trade and production, the necessity of usury, and the establishment of laws to protect individual profits and property from government and church interference. Ultimately, the bourgeois triumphed; medieval society was changed by the industrial revo-

lution, urbanization, the age of science and technology, capitalism, and the components that form contemporary society.[2]

The Reformed man was almost successful in ridding himself of the Gnostic view of the world—that false philosophy that had dominated medieval thought; but he could not shake loose the one teaching of Gnosticism that had caused the most havoc—Asceticism. Strangely enough, it was the ascetic lifestyle that brought about the accumulation of wealth. The Reformed man did not see the accumulation of wealth as wrong in itself, but with the accumulation of wealth came the problem of succumbing to it. John Wesley, the great Protestant preacher who lived during the early development of capitalism, wrote:

> I fear, wherever riches have increased, the essence of religion has decreased in the same proportion. Therefore, I do not see how it is possible, in the nature of things, for any revival of true religion to continue long. For religion must necessarily produce both industry and frugality, and these cannot but produce riches. But as riches increase, so will pride, anger, and love of the world in all branches. How then is it possible that Methodism, that is a religion of the heart, though it flourishes now as a green bay tree, should continue in this state? For the Methodists in every place grow diligent and frugal; consequently they increase in goods, in anger, in the desire of the flesh, the desire of the eyes, and the pride of life. So although the form of religion remains, the spirit is swiftly vanishing away. Is there no way to prevent this — this continual decay of pure religion? We ought not to prevent people from being diligent and frugal; we must exalt all Christians to gain all they can, and to save all they can; that is, in effect, to grow rich.[3]

Max Weber makes this astute observation about this early Protestant struggle:

> It was the same fate which again and again fell the predecessor of this world asceticism, the monastic asceticism of the Middle Ages. In the latter case, when rational economic activity had worked out its full effect by strict regulation of

conduct and limitation of consumption, the wealth accumulation either succumbed directly to the nobility as in the time
before the Reformation, or monastic discipline threatened
to break down, and one more reformation became necessary.
In fact, the whole history of monasticism is in a certain sense
the history of a continual struggle with the problem of the
secularizing influence of wealth.[4]

Capitalism not only has in it the seeds of gnosticism—it also has Judeo-
Christian traditions, which make it perhaps the most attractive economic system to Christians. John R. Richardson quotes Dr. Howard E.
Kershner as he explains the relationship between Christianity and capitalism:

> Christianity and capitalism are certainly not synonymous
> but there is a large measure of interdependence. Capitalism
> can develop also in a society of men which basically follows
> the Christian principles of honesty, integrity, truthfulness,
> fair play, and justice. Historically, capitalism did not develop
> until after Christian principles gained wide recognition. If
> Christianity declines, we believe capitalism and self-govern-
> ment will disappear. Christianity emphasizes the importance
> of the individual. Capitalism is the only economic system
> which exalts the individual and makes him superior to the
> group.[5]

Capitalism is by far the best of the world's economic systems, because it comes closest to the biblical mandates for financial success.
Capitalism thrives on the individuality and freedom of man. That in
itself gives evidence of biblical roots, for we read:

> And God said, Let us make man in our image, after our
> likeness: so God created man in his own image, in the image
> of God created he him; male and female created he them
> (Gen. 1:26, 27).

What makes man most like God is not a body—for God is a Spirit—
but man's ability to reason and think. God created man with the freedom to decide his own destiny. He can be saved or lost, rich or poor,

bound or free. It is, in the main, his choice. Capitalism allows man to exercise this God-given ability.

But what many Christians have done is bought into capitalism completely—as if capitalism were Christianity. Here is where the confusion and danger begin. As has been pointed out, capitalism is a mixture of truth and error—it is a system like any man-made system, riddled with injustices and inequities. Martin Luther King, Jr., in *Strides Toward Freedom*, pungently states:

> Capitalism is always in danger of inspiring man to be more concerned about making a living, than making a life. We are prone to judge success by the index of our salaries or the size of our automobiles, rather than by the quality of our service and relationship to humanity — thus capitalism can lead to practical materialism that is just as pernicious as the materialism taught by Communism.[6]

The weakness of capitalism has led to a paradox. Asceticism—which formed the basis of capitalism—in an attempt not to fall prey to a material world, gives way to a pragmatic materialism which is just as dangerous and Gnostic as asceticism itself. This pragmatic materialism of capitalism became a source of irritation, and the cause of a new economic system.

Communism, the second system, arose in reaction to the superfluous injustices that came about through the pragmatic materialism of capitalism. Adam Smith, the Scottish economist who had such great impact on twentieth-century economic thought, wrote that capitalistic philosophy was one of the causative factors of the abuses in a capitalistic society. George Gilder, in *Wealth and Poverty*, explains Smith's philosophy:

> Adam Smith was at once an intellectual who shared all the typical prejudices against the business class and a libertarian conservative who knew the value of freedom and enterprise. His solution was to locate the source of wealth not in the creative activities of business men but in the "invisible market." Smith believed that capitalism worked not because of

43

the virtues of capitalists but because of the "great machine" of exchange that converted their apparent greeds and vices into economic value. . . . "Businessmen may be vulgar and avaricious, full of childish vanities and selfish indulgences," said Smith; "seldom do they gather but to conspire against the public." But it was their very self-love, their avarice, their desire for self-indulgence that impelled the growth of economies. "Not from benevolence," wrote Smith in his famous lines, "do we expect bread from the baker . . . but from his self-love." In *The Theory of Moral Sentiments* he wrote that it is from the luxury and caprice of the rich man that we gain that share of the necessaries of life that we in vain have expected from his humanity. . . . In spirit of their natural selfishness and rapacity, though they mean only their own conveniency, though the sole end which they purpose from the labors of all the thousands they employ, be the gratification of their own vain and insatiable desires . . . they are led by an invisible hand . . . without intending it, without knowing it, to advance the society."[7]

But from the viewpoint of the exploited poor and their sympathizers, the invisible hand never worked, and injustices became worse. Karl Marx, a German revolutionary leader and socialist, became the leader of an opposition group against capitalism. His *Das Kapital* became the Communist bible and led to the organization of the Communist Party.

Communism may be defined as a social theory that undertakes to cure all social ills, especially those caused by capitalism. It seeks to accomplish this by completely reorganizing society. It is a revolutionary system that seeks to abolish all private ownership of property and place ownership in the hands of the state. Communism is simply a consistent form of socialism. In fact, socialism and communism only differ in the manner in which reform is brought about. Communism ascribes to force, while socialism votes the change.

Christians cannot ascribe to communism or socialism, because they both strike at a fundamental teaching of Christianity—the free will of man. In communism, a man cannot choose for himself. What is good for society is determined by men in charge of the higher echelons of government. But Christians must excoriate communism for still other reasons. Communism positions itself as an enemy of the church, the home, and even of God Himself. Karl Marx declared Christianity "an opiate of the people" and believed that Christianity and all other religions must be destroyed. Under Marx's influence, communist countries have sought to weed out Christianity. Communism seeks to destroy the church through the outlawing of religion, the banishing of pastors and priests, and the general persecution of those who profess a belief in God. As for the family, the Communist Party understands the strength derived from families, so in the Communist Manifesto we find this statement:

> On what foundation is the present family based? On capital, on private gain. In its completely developed form the family exists only among the bourgeoisie. But this state of things finds its complement in the practical absence of the family among the proletarians, and in public prostitution. The bourgeois family will vanish as a matter of course when its complement vanishes, and both will vanish with the vanishing of capital.[8]

Communism sought to accomplish the destruction of the home by teaching loyalty to the state rather than loyalty to parents. Children were no longer under the jurisdiction of parents but were wards of the state. Finally, Communism is anti-God and has organized men into societies of atheism. The Communist Party becomes the substitute for religion. The state becomes the people's God; the Communist Manifesto, their sacred book; and a classless society, their kingdom of God.

Despite Communism's totally anti-biblical foundation, some Christians are lured into believing and accepting some parts of this economic system. This happens because of misinterpreting the account of a communal setting in the book of Acts:

> And all that believed were together, and had all things common; And sold their possessions and goods, and parted them to all men as every man had need (Acts 2:44, 45).

Some have interpreted this text to be a reference to Communism. But a closer examination of the text reveals a caring church in a time of crisis. John Richardson, in explaining this text, quotes Rousas John Rusdoony, who says:

> The Communism of the early church, in Acts, was not economic in any sense, and should not be considered as an economic experiment. The church took seriously our Lord's prophecy concerning the coming fall of Jerusalem (Matthew 24). They knew that they were living in a doomed city and country. The logical step of faith was to make liquid their assets for ready flight. Some who made liquid their assets dedicated their funds in part or whole to the church, for the evangelization of Judea before its destruction. The relief money collected by Paul was not collected because of an economic experiment that had failed at Jerusalem and Judea. Men there continued in their vocations and simply lived in rented properties since their assets had been made liquid. The problem was a severe drought which had struck the entire area, creating a serious economic crisis and extreme shortage of food. This is a matter of historical record. Outside help was needed by virtually all in Judea, and the Christians were no exceptions. Thus, communism had nothing to do with it, and did not exist in the early church. Because the Christians were prepared for ready flight by our Lord's words, and by reason of having divested themselves of properties, none lost their lives in the fateful war with Rome, A.D. 66-70.[9]

Looking more closely at the text, we discover that the communal sharing was voluntary, not commanded by God, and that material goods were distributed according to the individual's needs. This is the opposite of communism. Communism is a forced sharing. The distribution is equal, but not equitable. Individual needs are never considered in communism. Every person receives the same, no matter what the need.

As we look at economic systems, we must evaluate them according to biblical principles. We must see the false philosophies that are part and parcel of those systems. Then we must seek to order our lives, not after or because of an economic system, but after the biblical principles that are always safe and true.

Notes:

1. Jeremy Rifkin and Ted Howard, *The Emerging Order* (New York, NY: G. P. Putnam & Sons, 1979), p. 21.

2. *Ibid.*, p. 22.

3. Max Weber, *The Protestant Ethic and the Spirit of Capitalism* (New York, NY: Charles Scribner & Sons, 1958), p. 175.

4. *Ibid.*, p. 174.

5. John R. Richardson, *Christian Economics* (Houston, TX: St. Thomas Press, 1966), p. 32.

6. Martin Luther King, Jr., *Strides Toward Freedom* (New York, NY: Harper & Row Publishers, 1964), p. 94.

7. George Gilder, *Wealth and Poverty* (New York: Basic Book Publisher, 1981), p. 36.

8. Richardson, p. 68.

9. *Ibid.*, p. 60.

THE TRUTH ABOUT WEALTH

We have examined two false ideologies that have influenced Christian thinking and have caused ambiguous thinking about the material world. Their errors have been set before us. To establish the tension that Socrates mentioned, which will lead us out of the valley of ambiguity to the mountain of truth, we must now explore the biblical view of the material world.

As we open the pages of Holy Writ, we are confronted with God at work in the creation of the world. James Welden Johnson, in his poem "Creator," says that after each planned creation, God shouted, "It is good" (Genesis 1).

R. C. Sproul, Jr., in his book *Money Matters*, sees the creation account as emphatically stating that "the material world is good."[1]

> More is involved with this judgment than the simple declaration that "God saw that it was good" (Gen. 1). Unlike the Greek, the Old Testament Jew viewed creation as a voluntary action of God. According to the Bible, the world did not evolve or emanate from eternal substance. Rather God chose to create it by divine decree. The implications of that for the value of material things are staggering. God chose to create a material world. He decided within the framework of his own divine mind, to make a world with food and drink and sex in it. Indeed he circumscribed the use of these physical things

by his righteous law. They were included in man's fall. They are integral parts of man's redemption.[2]

This doctrine of creation is fundamental to Christianity. All that we Christians hold dear hinges on the fact that God created the world. The fact that God is responsible for the existence of matter identifies Him as one who cares and is concerned. That in itself is a soothing message not only for clear thinking about the material world, but also for building our confidence that God will supply our material needs.

> The Christian doctrine of creation is the one great bulwark against all forms of idolatry common to paganism. Idolatry is the worship of what man has made or of some aspect of the creation. Matter is to be highly regarded and appreciated, but to God alone belongs worship. No part of the universe is to take the place of the Creator in our devotion.[3]

But the doctrine of Creation not only strikes at the root of idolatry, it also attacks asceticism. "Since God created all things and saw that they were good, created things can never be regarded as in themselves evil. That would lead to an asceticism which is completely foreign to the Bible."[4]

The earth and its bountiful resources are good, because they come from the hands of the holy and righteous God. A favorable view of the material world also can be derived from the doctrine of the incarnation. John writes, "The Word was made flesh and dwelt among us" (John 1:14). By this divine act of stepping out of eternity into time and garbing Himself in human flesh, Jesus has asserted for all time that the material world is good.

The Gnostic view that matter is inherently evil quite naturally led to a denial that Jesus had come in the flesh.

> For the Christian Gnostic, or for Christians influenced by Gnostic thought, the man Jesus of Nazareth was an embarrassment. The idea of the incarnation is a fundamental contradiction to their devaluation of the physical universe. It is unseemly, if not unthinkable, to assert that the Saviour of this world became flesh and dwelt among men as a real man. A human birth and particularly an ignominious suffering death

were not appropriate means to adopt in order to liberate men from the evils of physical birth, life, an interpretation of Christ developed which asserted that he did not really suffer and die, that he only appeared to do so. This is the position known as Docetism, from the Greek word for appear, or seem. Jesus' Passover was all play-action, a grand illusion.[5]

A sizeable group in the first century seems to have been influenced both by dualism and Docetism. The Docetist held that the human flesh in which Jesus appeared was fictitious. Redemption was drama, with a shadow for its hero. The phantom of a Redeemer was nailed to a phantom cross. Philosophical dualism became theological Docetism.

John wrote his epistles against the backdrop of Hellenistic culture, which has been greatly influenced by Oriental Gnosticism. As mentioned, early philosophies from the East and foreign heathen religion had amalgamated to produce a strong influence on all parts of society. Out of this grew the dualistic concepts which produced the Docetists. As a pastor first, John would naturally respond to influences that would lead his parishioners astray.

John's epistle appears to be a polemic against first-century Docetists. In his first epistle, he writes refuting the heresy of Docetism.

> That which was from the beginning, which we have heard, which we have seen with our eyes, which we looked upon, and our hands have handled of the Word of life; (for the life was manifested, and we have seen it, and bear witness and shew unto you that eternal life, which was with the Father, and was manifested unto us); that which we have seen and heard declare we unto you that ye also may have fellowship with us; and truly our fellowship is with the Father and with His Son Jesus Christ (I John 1:1-13).

John recognized the damage of Docetism, not only to the Christian worldview, but also to the reality of his salvation. He writes in warning:

> Beloved, believe not every spirit (teacher), but try the spirits whether they are of God: because many false prophets are gone out into the world, hereby, know ye the Spirit of God:

every spirit that confesseth not that Jesus Christ is come in the flesh is not of God: and this is that spirit of antichrist, whereof ye have heard that it should come, and even now is it in the world (I John 4:1-3).

The struggle between the biblical view of the incarnation and Docetism was a lethal one. John, seeking to deal a deadly blow to the heresy, wrote in his Gospel:

But one of the soldiers with a spear pierced his side, and forthwith came there out blood and water. And he that saw it bare record and his record is true; and he knoweth that he saith true, that ye might believe. Then saith he to Thomas, reach hither thy finger, and behold my hands; and reach thy hand, and thrust it into my side; and be not faithless, but believing (John 19:34, 35; 20:27).

These passages indicate that Christ was not a phantom, but a real person who could be seen, heard, and handled. Thomas was sure of Christ's resurrection on the basis of tangible, material evidence.

A few years ago William Temple said quite correctly, "Christianity is the most materialistic of all religions". . . . Temple pointed out that other religions had ignored matter, saying it is an illusion, that is does not really exist; and then he added, "Christianity based as it is on the incarnation, regards matter as destined to be the vehicle and instrument of spirit as fully factual as far as it controls and directs matter." Temple spoke of Christ as "the great materialist."[6]

It stands to reason, if in fact matter is evil, that a righteous God could never identify Himself with the material world, let alone become a part of it.

The final evidence that the biblical view of material is good is that of the creation of man. "And the Lord God formed man of the dust of the ground, and breathed into his nostrils the breath of life; and man became a living soul" (Genesis 2:7).

God, in stooping to put His hands into the dust of the earth and form man, demonstrated His affinity for the material world. But even greater evidence of God's approval of the material world is seen in His use of the material to make the crowning work of His creation: man. "That man is composed of materials derived from the ground, the elements of the earth, is confirmed by science. Decomposition of the human body after death bears witness to the same fact."[7]

Would God take material, dust from the earth, and mold and fashion it in His own image, if in fact it were evil?

God could have created man like an angel, a spiritual being, but instead He gave him a body. God created man from the earth and blessed him, putting His seal of approval upon him. We must listen to the words of the angel speaking to Peter in vision: "What God has pronounced pure, you must not call defiled" (Acts 10:15).

In summary, we can never expect to find biblical support for a devaluation of the human body or the material world in which human beings must live. There is plenty of support, both in the Old and New Testaments, for God's judgment concerning the misunderstanding and misuse of material. But the Bible never draws a dichotomy between the Spirit world and the material. It teaches that man needs the material as well as spiritual. Man is to use matter in the service of God, bringing blessing to himself, others, and the cause of God.

We now see the tension: the error of Gnosticism—and the truth that material is good. As Christians, we must choose Bible truth. Sproul says:

> The Greeks' future hope was redemption from the body. The Christian's hope is redemption of the body. The Greek viewed the body as the prison, house of the soul. The Christian views the body as the temple of the Holy Spirit. The Greek viewed material things as being intrinsically imperfect. The Christian views them as good things created by God, though capable of sinful use and abuse.[8]

Notes:

1. R. C. Sproul, Jr., *Money Matters* (Wheaton, IL: Tyndale House Publishers, 1985), p. 24.

2. *Ibid.*

3. John R. Richardson, *Christian Economics* (Houston, TX: St. Thomas Press, 1966), p. 6.

4. Reginald H. Fuller and Brian K. Rice, *Christianity and the Affluent Society* (Grand Rapids, MI: William B. Eerdmans Publishing Company, 1966), p. 12.

5. Marianne H. Micks, *Introduction Theology* (New York: Seabury Press, Inc. 1967), p. 74.

6. Richardson, p. 7.

7. *Seventh-day Adventist Bible Commentary*, Isaiah to Malachi, vol. 4 (Washington, D.C.: Review and Herald Publishing Association, 1955), p. 222.

8. Sproul, p. 25.

WEALTH AND THE 3-D MAN

The Bible clearly defines the different dimensions of man. "Beloved, I wish above all things that you prosper and be in good health, even as thy soul prospereth" (3 John 2).

The different dimensions are the spiritual, physical, and material. Even though the dimensions can be singled out, they cannot be separated. Each dimension is a part of the whole, yet none can function alone. John, in the passage above, shows the interrelationship of the parts by stating that as one area improves, so do the others. The converse is implied—that if one is impoverished, so are the others.

Again we see the Bible trampling down any ideology that smacks of other-worldliness. God never intended nor intends for us to be "so heavenly minded that we are no earthly good." He reveals the importance of a balanced life.

Man is pictured in this text as a triangle. If one side is removed, the triangle is incomplete. All sides are needed to make the triangle. Please note how these three facets of man integrate, as shown in the diagram at the top of the following page:

Another illustration of this passage is that of balance. Life must be lived with the material and the physical being balanced on the fulcrum of spirituality.

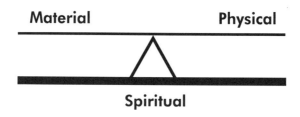

If the scales are tipped too far in any direction, or the fulcrum removed, disaster will occur. When we tilt the scale in favor of the material, we become materialists. Material things become our god. We contradict Christ, who said, "for a man's life consisteth not in the abundance of things which he possesseth" (Luke 12:15).

If the scales weigh out too much in favor of the physical, then we may become walking health zombies or hypochondriacs. But many Christians have sought to live life with just the fulcrum, or spiritual. That's why we have spent time earlier in this book explaining the heresy that leads to this type of lifestyle. There can be no spiritual life without the physical and material.

Cecil A. Ray, in *Living the Responsible Life*, says, "Material things are essential to man. This is God's plan. Man requires the benefits of material things for the care of his mind, and for the balance of his emotions."[1]

When viewing man from this holistic standpoint, we understand that our response to the material world should be positive. We see ourselves as valuable in God's scheme of things. The material world is seen as a gift of God for the needs of life.

Notice the sequence of creation (Genesis 1). God creates the complete material world: sun, moon, trees, vegetables, animals, etc. Then,

> God said unto them [Adam and Eve], be fruitful, and multiply, and replenish the earth, and subdue it, and have dominion over the fish of the sea, and over the fowl of the air, and over every living thing that moveth upon the earth (Gen. 1:27).

This was God's divine directive for our response to the earth:

> Man is the climax of God's creation. He is made from the earth, an earthling. This gives him a close tie to the earth. He is a part of the created world and shares many common needs with the rest of creation. Yet, man is different, quite different. By the choice of God, he is set apart from the rest of creation. That which makes him different is his being made "in the image of God." The Bible does not indicate that any other part of creation is given this rare distinction. It is only of man. God personally fashions man from the earth and imparts to him his own breath.[2]

Harold Lindsell, in *Free Enterprise—A Judeo-Christian Defense*, writes:

> Throughout the Old and New Testaments, the writers proclaimed that it was the intention of God for all people to enjoy his creation. Plentiful provision was made for people to use what God has created. What is called the "Creation Mandate" was charge to all human life to create wealth.... God gave the earth and all of its fullness to mankind for their use as stewards. Any failure to use what God has provided is no less wrong than the misuse of God's creation. Within the boundaries set by God, people were free and free today to do as they please.[3]

Lindsell adds to the creation mandate our responsibility of proper stewardship. In other words, our response to the material is not simply to enjoy it, but also to manage it. *Stewardship* is a biblical term. In both Old and New Testaments, the concept of stewardship is found. In Genesis 14:2 we find Eleazar being named the steward of Abraham's house. The Hebrew word *Usar* is used to express Eleazar's position. *Sar* means head person and manager. In the New Testament, the Greek words *epitro-pos*, meaning "manager," and *oikonomous*, meaning "overseer," are both used to express stewardship. So we can see that both the Old and New Testaments convey the same concept of a steward—one who manages or supervises the affairs of another. The word *stewardship* is used three times in the Bible (Luke 16:2, 3, 4).

The word *steward*—the root word of *stewardship*—is used seventeen times: Genesis 15:2, 43, 19; 44:1; 44:4; 1 Kings 16:9; Matthew 20:8; Luke 8:3, 12:42, 16:1-3, 7, 8; Titus 1:7; 1 Chronicles 28:1; 1 Corinthians 4:1, 2; 1 Peter 4:10.

The word *stewardship* comes from two Greek words: *oikos*, meaning "house," and *nomos*, meaning "law." Literally, the word *stewardship* means "house-law." W. E. Vines states, "Oikonomia primarily signifies the management of a household or of household affairs; then the management or administration of the property of others."[4]

We are called by God to be managers of His majestic and magnificent world. We are God's stewards.

> It is no secret that many people are "turned off" and "out" by the very mention of Christian stewardship. This is true because they have heard the word used almost entirely with reference to financial campaigns and request of money. Homes Roston is right when he says that for many people, stewardship means only a "thinly veiled attempt to separate them from their money."[5]

It is unfortunate that the church has perpetrated this view of stewardship, but we should never allow that to dampen our respect and admiration for the role God has called us to fill in response to His word. If we do, we will never enter richly into the understanding of our relationship to God, His world, Jesus Christ, and mankind, that can come from Christian stewardship. Neither will we ever know the real joy of being one of God's managers.

Christian stewardship is managing faithfully the material world within the boundaries set by God. Paul, in his epistle to the Corinthians, writes, "It is required in stewardship that a man be found faithful" (1 Corinthians 4:2).

Notes:

1. Cecil A. Ray, *Living the Responsible Life* (Nashville: Convention Press, 1974), p. 8.

2. *Ibid.*, p. 4.

3. Harold Lindsell, *Free Enterprise —A Judeo-Christian Defense* (Illinois: Tyndale House Publishers, Inc., 1982), pp. 70-71.

4. W. E. Vines, *An Exposition Dictionary of New Testament Words* (Old Tappan, NY: Fleming H. Revell Company, 1940), p. 320.

5. Turner H. Clinard, *Responding to God* (Philadelphia, PA: Westminster Press, 1980), p. 32.

BIBLICAL LAWS FOR WEALTH-BUILDING

We have defined a steward as one who manages another's property. Managers will always have rules or laws laid down by the owner for proper management of his property. In fact, in the original word for *stewardship* is the word *law*.

We are three-dimensional, and every dimension is regulated by the laws of God. Our spiritual dimension is regulated by the moral law of Exodus 20:8-11; our physical, by health laws found in Leviticus 11 and Deuteronomy 14. God operates in an orderly fashion, with rules and laws. This can be clearly seen in nature, where we observe the law of gravity, the law of aerodynamics, the law of sowing and reaping.

Therefore, we must conclude that God does not leave our economic well-being to chance but regulates it too by laws. The Bible is not a book of economics, but it reveals laws to govern our economy.

I choose to think in terms of laws, because this turns the management of the material world into a serious matter. Some Christian writers choose to view biblical economic guidelines as simply God's suggested better way for us, leaving the impression that one might be financially free and prosperous without them.

Fear is present in owning up to a God who commands. Law is never evil or against man. God's established laws are for the good of the world. He created us and the world, and laws are His means of telling how best to use His property. The Old Testament declares a God of both blessings and cursings.

If we obey Him, blessings will come; but if we break His commands, we must suffer the consequences. This is seen in a practical way in nature:

> For example, when one learns to live in harmony with gravity he can use it to great advantage. He can enjoy the fun of skiing or bobsledding. He can coast down a hill on his bicycle. He can use inclined planes to ease his work of lifting. He can place furniture on a floor and expect it to remain in place. However, if he attempts to violate the law of gravity in flying by flapping his hands in the air, he will have a rude shock when he hits the ground.[1]

The eternal laws of economics are similar. As any man understands and lives in harmony with them, he will succeed. Just as certainly, violations of these laws will end in disaster.

The Law of Ownership

The first law is the law of ownership. Remember, we are simply managers. "All of us as Christians are members of the greatest company in the world. God started this business. . . "[2] No one makes a good manager unless he remembers who owns the business.

The Bible unequivocally says that God owns everything in this world: "The earth is the Lord's and the fullness thereof; the world, and they that dwell therein" (Psalm 24:1).

Universal ownership—that is God's claim. And beyond saying that in a general way, He is specific about it. "The silver is mine, and the gold is mine, saith the Lord of host" (Hag. 2:8). "For every beast of the forest is mine, and the cattle upon a thousand hills . . . and the beasts of the field are mine" (Psalm 50:10, 11). Yes, God owns the business.

The method God chooses to test obedience to this law is tithing.

Tithing may be defined as devoting one-tenth of one's increase to the service of God. The term tithe itself means "one-tenth."[3]

God instructs:

> And all the tithe of the land, whether of the sea or the land, or the fruit of the tree, is the Lord's; it is holy unto the Lord. And concerning the tithe of the land, or of the flock, even of whatsoever passeth under the rod, the tenth shall be holy unto the Lord (Lev. 27:30, 32).

God calls for the tithe, not because He needs it, but because it is so easy for a manager to get "my-itis." We think that because of hard and diligent work, all that we have is ours. It's *my* house, *my* car, *my* boat, *my* . . . *my* . . .

Moses warned:

> Beware that thou forget not the Lord thy God,... lest when thou hast eaten and art full, and hast built goodly houses, and dwelt therein; and thou say in thine heart, my power and the might of mine hand hath gotten me this wealth (Deut. 8:11-12:17).

By returning to God the firstfruits of our labor, we show in a tangible way that "all good and perfect gifts come from above" (James 1:17).

God has given us the full run of His business, and all that He requires is simply a tithe. But many get testy about what they have in their possession and refuse to honor the law of ownership. What would you do if you owned a store and the manager refused to turn over to you the profits? Of course, you would fire him and hire someone else. It is a small wonder that God hasn't fired many more of us. No one will have financial freedom while violating this law.

The first mention of tithing is in the first book of the Bible. Abraham presented a tithe to Melchizedek after returning from the rescue of his nephew Lot (Gen. 14:30). This shows that tithing preceded the nation of Israel. The law applies to all who expect to prosper financially. Israel violated this law, and the whole nation suffered greatly as a result. God sent the prophet Malachi with these words:

Will a man rob God? Yet ye have robbed me. But ye say, wherein have we robbed thee? In tithes and offerings (Mal. 3:8).

Malachi charged the whole nation of Israel with the sin of being thieves and robbers in the sight of God. He recognized that the calamities of Israel were due to their failure to bring the tithe to God. Their failure to tithe was proof that they had backslidden, forgetting that God owns everything and that they were just managers.

In a sermon preached in the year A.D. 398, John Chrysostom said, "If it were dangerous for the Jews to fail in giving tithes then surely it must be much more dangerous now."[4]

Malachi instructed Israel to return from breaking this law:

Bring ye all the tithes into the storehouse, that there may be meat in mine house, and prove me now herewith, saith the Lord of hosts (Mal. 3:10).

Again, the law of ownership is seen through the tithe. It is a law, and there are benefits when the law is obeyed and curses when it is violated. Malachi elucidates the consequences of violating this law: "Ye are cursed with a curse" (Mal. 3:9). God does not actually curse us when we break the ownership law, but He allows us to suffer the consequences of not being blessed by Him.

Those who feel that they cannot afford to tithe are looking only at one side of the coin. The other side is whether they can afford to miss any of God's blessings in their lives, their families, or their businesses. It is not that God withholds blessing, but rather that He cannot add further blessings apart from our action.[5]

But just as there are curses, there are blessings. Malachi shares with us the blessing of adhering to the law of ownership in these words:

Bring all your tithes into the storehouse so that there will be food enough in my Temple. If you do, I will open up the windows of heaven for you and pour out a blessing so great you won't have room enough to take it in! Try it! Let me prove it to you. Your crops will be large, for I will guard them from insects and plagues. Your grapes won't shrivel away before they ripen, says the Lord of Hosts (Mal. 3:10-11; Living Bible).

Obeying God does pay off—not just after a while, but here and now. Before long, as one obediently honors God through his tithe, he is made into the pleasant giver described in 2 Cor. 9:7: "For God loveth a cheerful giver."

The Law of Investing

The second law given in the Bible for financial freedom is the law of investing. According to *Webster's New World Dictionary*, investing is "putting money into business, real estate, stocks, bonds, etc., for the purpose of obtaining an income or profit."[6] All owners expect their businesses to earn a profit, and the same is true for God. He expects us, His managers, to invest wisely the things He has entrusted to us. But God wants us not only to invest, but also to turn a profit.

The word "profit" today has a bad ring to it. It has become a six-letter obscenity. Just as "rugged individualism" has turned individualism into an ugly word, so also adjectives like "indecent," "exploitive," and "obscene" have made the word "profit" a bad taste.[7]

Profit is simply deriving some gain from an investment. Jesus taught in a number of ways the importance of a profit. Perhaps the most familiar example is the parable of the talents. The parable is recorded in Matthew's Gospel and goes like this:

A talent was a sum of money, equal perhaps to $1,000 or more. When the lord left his country for a long visit abroad, he left his money in care of his servants for investment. They became stewards and business partners by virtue of their trust. He recognized that they did not all have equal ability, so he left to each servant an amount for investment that he felt he could handle, and took his journey. The man with $5,000 invested his trust and earned $5,000 more; and the man with $2,000 earned $2,000 more. But the man with $1,000 hid his money in a hole in the ground.[8]

For the servants who invested, the lord had a commendation, but for the noninvesting servant, severe words and punishment were meted out.

Who can operate a business long without making a profit? Jesus says, "Ye shall know them by their fruits [profits]" (Matt. 7:16). The disciples learned the importance of profits in Jesus' parable about the fig tree:

> A certain man had a fig tree planted in his vineyard; and he came out and sought fruit thereon, and found none. Then said the dresser of his vineyard, behold, these three years I come seeking fruit on this fig tree, and find none; cut it down, why cumbereth it the ground? And he answering said unto him, lord, let it alone this year also, till I shall dig about it, and dung it; and if it bear fruit, well, and if not, then after that thou shalt cut it down (Luke 13:6-9).

Jesus here emphatically states the importance of a gain on investment. Matthew says it this way: "And, cast the unprofitable servant into outer darkness" (Matt. 25:30).

Back to our illustration of the manager of the business. The owner commissions the manager to invest wisely the goods in his store so that a profit will be realized. If no profit is realized, the owner will look for a manager who can produce a gain.

But where should the manager invest? There are many places we may invest, such as real estate, stocks, bonds, mutual funds, savings bonds, commodities, gold, and silver. All of these investments are good, but all have a degree of risk. Real estate can be a good investment, but if the location is bad or goes bad after you have purchased it, it could be a losing investment. You can buy gold, but if the price goes low, you can lose. The manager's job is to pick out the best investment, understanding that the higher the risk, the greater the returns; the lower the risk, the lower the returns.

The wise investor protects his owner's investment by looking for the lowest-risk, highest-yield investment possible. He settles not for the better, but the best. The best investment is a no-risk, high-yield investment. Where can you find that kind of investment? Jesus gives this advice about investing:

> Lay not up for yourselves treasures upon earth, where moth and rust doth corrupt, and where thieves break through and steal. But lay up for yourselves treasures in heaven, where neither moth nor rust doth corrupt, and where thieves do not break through nor steal. But seek you first the kingdom of God (Matt. 6:19-20, 33).

This text is not meant to condemn investing in any of the earlier-mentioned investments, but serves as a passage to help us prioritize our investments.

Our largest investment ought to be where we will receive the greatest return. As managers, our greatest investment should be in heaven. How can we invest in heaven? If we were to tie up our money in a handkerchief and throw it as high as we could, it wouldn't reach but a few feet into the sky, let alone heaven. Even in the technological age of space shuttles, we still couldn't get our money up to heaven. How then do we invest in heaven? Again, Jesus speaks, "Verily, I say unto you, in as much as ye did not to one of the least of these, ye did it not unto me" (Matt. 25:45). Jesus refers to our responsibility to minister to the less fortunate as a way of investing in His kingdom. As we minister to the needs of humanity with our resources, we are investing in the Kingdom of God.

Solomon describes the returns on this heavenly investment: "The liberal soul shall be made fat, and he that watereth shall be watered also himself" (Prov. 11:25).

How much should we invest? Even though God was specific about the amount given to obey the law of ownership, He left the decision of how much to invest up to us. There is a hint as to a goal we should set for ourselves in Mal. 3:8. Notice God brings down scathing remarks on Israel because she had robbed Him of tithe and offerings. We understand that the tithe is an outward sign of obedience to the law of ownership, but what is the offering? It is that portion used for investment. Notice that the coordinating conjunction "and" ties tithe and offerings together. A coordinating conjunction usually joins together things of equal value.[9] Since tithe is ten percent, the investment goal should be at least ten percent.

But God doesn't legislate on the investment. He is concerned with us using our cognitive reasoning. If God told us every single thing to do, we would no longer be managers; we would be robots. So the decision of how much to invest is left to our discretion, with some guidelines.

There are some questions we may ask ourselves as we make the decision on how much to invest:

1. How much profit do I want to make?

2. How much do I trust God?

3. How rapidly do I want the Kingdom of God to grow?

The children of Israel took the law of investing seriously and invested a full twenty-three percentage points above the tithe in the cause of God.[10] It would seem that such a large amount invested would bring Israel to poverty. But they understood that investing in God's Kingdom is a no-risk, high-yield investment. Their investments made them the most prosperous nation on the face of the earth.

The Law of Prudence

The third biblical law of economics is the law of prudence. This law is often neglected because of its seeming unimportance. Some faithfully obey the law of ownership and the law of investing but fail to adhere to this third and final law. James, the Apostle, had an inspired insight into the importance of obeying God completely. He writes, "for whosoever shall keep the whole law, and yet offend in one point, he is guilty of all" (James 2:10). It is clear from the context that this passage refers to the moral law of God. However, what is true for one of God's laws is true for them all. A simple illustration best establishes this point.

Consider health laws. These laws include proper rest, proper diet, adequate exercise, and plenty of sunshine. Now, a person could get adequate exercise, eat balanced meals, and play on the beach to get plenty of sunshine, but if he refused to allow his body to rest, he would soon die from exhaustion. Breaking just that one part of the law would bring his demise. Breaking just one of the economic laws can also lead to our financial demise. It ends up as if we had not obeyed any of the laws.

Webster defines *prudence* as "capable of exercising sound judgment in practical matters, sensible, wise, careful management."[11] The law of prudence is the wise management of that which is left over after tithe and offerings. It is handling that which is left for personal use with discretion. Leroy Brownlow, in *God's Plan for Financial Success*, writes:

> The God who made us, knowing the best way for us to live, taught us to be frugal and thrifty. Yet this basic principle of life is presently being scorned. Today there are many who think economy is almost a social crime. This shows how far our society has swung away from the old self-preserving principles set forth by the Creator.[12]

Many have ended up financially shipwrecked because they failed to live frugally. Solomon, the wise man, expressed the law of prudence in these words, "There is treasure to be desired and oil in the dwelling of the wise, but a foolish man spendeth it up" (Prov. 21:20). This passage distinguishes the wise and the foolish by calling attention to their spending habits. A faithful steward is one who not only knows who owns everything and is a good investor, but who is also conscientious about all the property of the owner.

There are three basic instructions for being prudent. The first instruction is to set financial goals. The importance of setting goals would seem obvious to most people. But the truth of the matter is that most people—especially Christians—do not set financial goals for themselves. Most Christians use God as an excuse for not setting goals. They passively say, "Trust God." Yes, it is of utter importance that we learn how to trust God, but trusting God should never take away the part we play in using our heads. The writer of the book of James says, "Faith without works is dead" (James 2:17). We must blend our trust in God with our personal goals; then we can expect financial success.

Goals are important, for they determine our destiny. The only way to accomplish anything is to set goals. Can you image a basketball game being played without baskets, or a football game being played without goal posts? So, we cannot expect to have financial freedom or success without setting goals. Goals are objects or ends that we strive to obtain. They are mental pictures of what we want and where we want to go in life.

> Goals are not dreams. They are human hopes that are clear and categorical, practical and powerful. And as a person acts upon his goals, his goals act upon him. They are absolutely necessary to success.[13]

Every person should have long- and short-term goals. These goals should be written goals, providing a visible and objective standard to work toward. It is beyond the scope of this book to go into a description of long- and short-range goals. But remember this—you won't hit anything if you never aim.

Once goals have been set, we must then learn how to budget—the second instruction for being prudent. A prudent person is one who understands that money has no sense. He knows that it is best to tell his money where to go, not to try to figure out where it went. This can only be done by budgeting. Budgeting is simply a plan for managing money—the method by which we reach our financial goals. Larry Burkett, in *The Financial Planning Workbook*, explains how most people feel about budgeting, "To many people, the word budgeting has a bad ring. Why? Because they see budgeting as a punishment plan."[14]

But really, budgeting is just the opposite of a punishment plan. It is actually a way of getting the things we really want. It is the way to financial freedom.

Everyone desires financial freedom. But freedom never comes without restriction. That is what budgeting is all about. It is restricting our desires to fit into our incomes. A car is free to be driven as long as it is restricted by the steering linkage. A kite will fly long and high as long as there is a restrictive string. And we are free to provide for our material and physical needs as long as we live on a budget.

Why is it so difficult to live on a budget? To answer that question, we must view budgeting in the light of the nature of man. Man came perfect from the hand of God. Every part of him was under control. But after his fall, man lost dominion not only of the earth, but also of himself. Augustine called this the original sin, and taught:

> Man and the angels possessed a freedom either to accept the order of Creation in which they existed, or to rebel. Some angels rebelled and then seduced man. Since submission to the order of creation would have meant self-fulfillment, rebellion against it necessarily involved the loss of the happiness of those who fulfill their own essential nature. The creatures were self-condemned to ignorance and to insatiable desire and concupiscence. The order which should have been obtained between reason and passion was disturbed and man found himself prey to every passing fancy and mood.[15]

For there is a struggle going on. The apostle Paul describes it this way:

> For I know that in me (that is, in my flesh), dwelleth no good thing: to will is present with me; but how to perform that which is good I find not. For the good that I would I do not; but the evil which I would not, that I do. Now if I do that I would not, it is no more I that do it, but sin that dwelleth in me. For I delight in the law of God after the inward man: But I see another law in my members warring against the law of my mind, and bringing me into captivity to the law of sin which is in my members (Rom. 7:19-23).

What clearer evidence of this struggle than in our personal finances? We find it so easy to live an impulsive life, buying what we don't need and failing to take care of the most important things. The struggle to live on a budget is difficult but not impossible. Paul again writes:

> But I keep under my body, and bring it into subjection: lest that by any means, when I have preached to others, I myself should be a cast away (1 Cor. 9:27).

Paul understood that the struggle can only be won by a concerted effort to control and restrict uncontrollable desires. Our hope of winning the financial struggle is only by living within the framework of a budget.

When establishing a budget, both husband and wife should be involved. This will give the budget a balanced dimension. Women tend to be pragmatists, while men are futurists. The typical husband plans the budget with a five-year view in mind, while the wife sees—and plans for—today's bills and needs. The two working together bring about a balance. Furthermore, working together eliminates much of the accusation that comes when the budget doesn't balance. When children reach the age of understanding what money is all about, they too should be included in the monthly budget sessions. This teaches them not only how to budget, but also the value of things.

This chapter was not written as a how-to for budgeting, but to show the importance and struggle of budgeting.

Budgeting can become a great aid to managing money efficiently, so we must not look at it as a nuisance or a necessary evil, but as a user-friendly guide to better living.

Budgeting:

1. Gives direction to family goals.

2. Places control on spending—keeping you out of debt.

3. Brings peace of mind—you know you've done your best.

4. Provides for emergencies.

The third instruction for being prudent is avoiding prodigality. In an affluent society, wastefulness has become a part of the general lifestyle. Our Lord demonstrated how He felt about wastefulness in the feeding of the five thousand. "Gather up the fragments that remain, that nothing be lost" (John 6:12). Jesus gave an example of what we should do with the ends of bread, the leftovers from dinner, and all the things that seem insignificant to us. Wastefulness is like a leak in a ship. A little leak can sink a ship just as surely as a big one. Too many end up financially sunk because of little leaks due to wastefulness.

One of the saddest and most pathetic stories in all the Bible is that of the Prodigal Son. After this young man demanded and secured his inheritance, he went "into a far country, and there wasted his substance in riotous living. And when he spent all, there arose a mighty famine in the land and he began to be in want" (Luke 15:13-14). Leroy Brownlow says this about this parable:

> Willful waste brings woeful want. And in this case the want was extremely woeful and wretched. He was reduced to the low level of hog pen living and desired even the husks which the swine refused to eat. Three key economic thoughts in the story are: (1) "wasted his substance," (2) "when he had spent all," and (3) "began to be in want." It just works that way. Waste and want go together and cannot be separated long.[16]

Few men have failed financially who have been conscious of their wastefulness. The prudent Christian will set financial goals, budget the money with which the Lord has blessed him, and not be wasteful.

Notes:

1. Douglas Anderson, Jr., *Owe No Man Anything* (Hampshire: Light and Salt, 1980), p. 44.

2. Turner H. Clinard, *Responding to God* (Philadelphia: Westminster Press, 1980), p. 37.

3. John R. Richardson, *Christian Economics* (Houston: St. Thomas Press, 1966), p. 130.

4. *Ibid.*, p. 132.

5. Ron Hembree, *You and Your Money* (Grand Rapids: Baker Book House, 1980), p. 116.

6. *Webster's New World Dictionary of the American Language* (1968), s.v. "Investing."

7. R. C. Sproul, Jr., *Money Matters* (Wheaton, IL: Tyndale House Publishers, 1985), p. 49.

8. Clinard, p. 38.

9. H. H. Dunbar, M. E. Marcett, and F. H. McCloskey, *A Complete Guide to Good Writing* (New York: D. C. Heath & Company, 1951), p. 45.

10. John White, *The Golden Cow* (Downers Grove, IL: Inter-Varsity Press, 1979), p. 23.

11. *Webster's*, s.v. "prudence."

12. Leroy Brownlow, *God's Plan for Financial Success* (Ft. Worth: Brownlow Publishing Company, Inc., 1979), p. 29.

13. *Ibid.*, p. 52.

14. Larry Burkett, *The Financial Planning Workbook* (Chicago: The Moody Press, 1982), p. 9.

15. Van A. Harvey, *Handbook of Theological Terms* (New York: Macmillan Publishing Co., Inc., 1964), p. 222.

16. Brownlow, p. 70.

Four Steps to Freedom From Guilt About Wealth

What you have discovered in *Wealth Without Guilt* is how this guilt complex about prosperity has become such an intimate part of our philosophy of life. But let me end this book with positive things you can do to shake loose from guilt about wealth.

Step 1—Accept Your Birthright of Prosperity

Most of the guilt we suffer about wealth is largely because of ignorance about our birthright as children of God. We were born to enjoy prosperity. Believe that! Accept that! Open your Bible daily and find and read two or three promises that focus on God's blessings. Fresh promises like these will purge your mind of the false idea that God wants you to live in poverty or from hand to mouth.

The order of creation, as mentioned earlier, is God's clear declaration of what He wants and desires for us. After six days of creating, God made man. From the very hand of God came His crowning masterpiece—human beings. As a testament of man's unique and special place in all creation, God created him in His own image and placed him in a prosperous garden home, commanding the first man and woman to have dominion over it.

Our original home was a place of plenty. God wants no less for us today. You and I are the greatest of His creation. Believe me when I tell you, God doesn't want us to live in poverty. It is not His plan for you to eke out a living. It is not His plan for you to live from paycheck to paycheck. Never allow anyone to convince you that God is satisfied with mere survival living for you. Survival living is for the birds—not for beings created in the image of God.

A daily reading of the Bible uproots one of the most devastating philosophies of all times—evolution. Evolution keeps us ignorant about our origins. And when we are ignorant of our origins, we are ignorant of our birthright. In fact, we don't even expect a birthright. Evolution allows us to settle for survival living. It puts us into competition with all other creatures God has made. It strips us of our high position in all of God's creation. We may act like monkeys at times, but we didn't come from monkeys—and neither should we expect to live like monkeys.

Many things in life are difficult or impossible to explain, but we know that there are no accidents or happenstances with God. Ignorance about our origins has fueled our guilt complex. We were created by God. Now, we must accept our birthright of prosperity. Just as we accept good health as God's plan for our lives, we must just as readily accept prosperity as His plan for us.

Of course, that doesn't mean that life will not have its up and downs. It doesn't mean that we all will be millionaires. But it does mean that even in the midst of the struggle, we can know that God's plan and desire for our lives is beyond the economic struggle and doesn't include poverty.

Step 2—Put the Blame Where It Belongs

God has taken a black eye because of how poverty has become such an accepted part of the Christian message. But God is not the Author of poverty. The story of Job clearly identifies the author of poverty, sickness, suffering, and death (see Job 1). Satan is the one who brought poverty and suffering to righteous Job—and to the world. Yet the blame has been laid at God's doorstep.

Without thinking it through, many of us today point the finger at

God for our financial struggles. We justify this unwarranted blame by saying that God is testing us. God does indeed know how to bring good out of bad things that happen. But He is not therefore the Author of the bad.

So Step 2 is to stop blaming God for your financial dilemma. Once the blame is placed in its rightful place, you can starting fighting financial woes just as you fight physical woes. When you are physically ill, you don't blame God and go around feeling guilt about being sick. You start working immediately to get well.

So get the monkey off your back. Sit down and write out where you would like to be financially, then every day do something to improve your financial condition. Pray David's prayer daily: "Pray for the peace of Jerusalem: they shall prosper that love thee. Peace be within thy walls, and prosperity within thy palaces" (Psalm 122:6, 7).

Step 3—Don't Look for Independence—but for Interdependence

It is so easy to misundertand the purpose of wealth. TV commercials, advertisements, and the "lifestyles of the rich and famous" have distorted our understanding of wealth. For many, the purpose of wealth is to give them freedom to be and do whatever they want. Wealth is thus their title to independence. But wealth is not given to make us independent—but rather interdependent.

To be sure, there is a type of freedom and independence that comes with wealth. That freedom is the independence to act more responsibly before God and man. God does not look with favor on the arrogance, self-sufficiency, and independence modeled by many among the affluent. Wealth should never be desired or sought after for the primary reason of asserting one's independence. In fact, wealth should tie us closer to humanity. The Scripture says, "To whom much is given, much is required."

Paul understood this concept. "I am a debtor to all men," he said. Every blessing is designed to draw us closer to Christ and to other people. True wealth humbles us. We realize that it was not in our own power that we received it. God has given wealth to us for a purpose—and that purpose is to bless humanity. The needs of humanity cry out. Guilt follows when we don't reach out and answer the cry of those in need with the wealth that we have.

Recently, I met a Christian man whom God has blessed tremendously. Rising from abject poverty in one of the poorest countries in the world, he has become one of the truly wealthy men of that country. Yet he walks the street ministering to the down and out. He owns a dozen orphanages all over the world. On his visits to these homes, he cuddles the children in his arms. These are the children he has rescued from life on city streets. These are the children of prostitutes, drug addicts, the homeless, the rejected. His wealth makes it impossible for him to be independent. He sees their needs—which become his needs. They need him, but he also needs them. In being one with the people and meeting their needs, any burden of guilt about wealth is lifted.

Step 4—Decide When Enough Is Enough

Guilt comes from the the abuse, misuse, and waste of wealth. Wealth given by God brings with it responsibility and accountability. God will not allow a person to abuse wealth without experiencing guilt. This guilt is God's way of bringing us back to faithful stewardship.

Perhaps this step is the most difficult to take in a society that places so much value on things. In this affluent age of ours, we are made to feel that the purpose of wealth is for display ("If you've got it, flaunt it," the saying goes). Therefore many, in a feeble attempt to prove their worth, waste their wealth. But the waste of wealth, instead of adding value to one's life, adds guilt.

This final step encourages you to put a cap on your lifestyle. Make a prayerful effort to set limits to your spending and buying. Determine to live as simple a life as possible. This by no means encourages or supports the ascetic life mentioned earlier. It just means that you don't clutter your life with things. It means that you have opted out of the game called "He who dies with the most toys wins." Simplicity is a different matter for everyone. Deciding what is enough for you should never dictate what is enough for someone else. Your limits should be set by your true family needs, with prayerful direction from God. Here are some things to take into consideration when making that decision:

1. Remember that you can only sleep in one bed at a time, drive one car at a time, and live in one house at a time.

2. Remember that no matter how much you get, material things will never provide security.

3. Remember that the more you accumulate, the more time, energy, and resources will be required not only to secure them, but to maintain them.

4. Remember that the more you accumulate, the more material things tend to separate you from other people.

What makes it so tough to take this final step is that the entire economic system is based on people never being satisfied. The very rubric of our human economy is wastefulness, abuse, and indulgence. So to take this final step, you must change your philosophy of life. You must find a new economy—an economy that encourages responsible living and faithful stewardship. In my book, *Theo-Economics—The Call to Responsibility*, a new economic system is introduced. It is a system that allows a man to have wealth without fear, frustration, or guilt.

The path to guilt-free living about wealth will always have its struggles, because the devil wants to keep you believing that you are a pauper, when you are really a child of the king. You will need to retrace your steps often to make sure the monkey of guilt is off your back. My prayer is that God will constantly prosper you, so that the kingdom of Grace will soon become His eternal kingdom.

OTHER BOOKS BY DR. ROLAND J. HILL

Theo-Economics

Money—The Acid Test

How to Get Out of Debt (workbook)

For pricing and ordering information, contact the author at . . .

Helping Hands Press
P.O. Box133
Keene, TX 76059
Phone: (817) 645-3258
Fax: (817) 558-1589